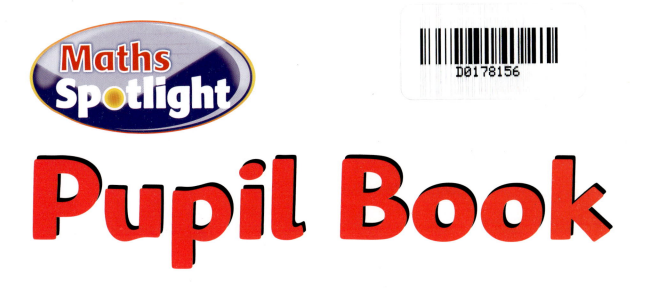

Maths Spotlight

Pupil Book

4

D0178156

Heinemann

Series editor	Peter Clarke
Consultant	Len Frobisher
Writing team	Janine Blinko
	Paula Coombes
	Hilary Koll
	Steve Mills
	Jeanette Mumford

Heinemann is an imprint of Pearson Education Limited, a company incorporated in England and Wales, having its registered office at Edinburgh Gate, Harlow, Essex, CM20 2JE. Registered company number: 872828
www.heinemann.co.uk

Heinemann is a registered trademark of Pearson Education Ltd

© Harcourt Education Ltd 2002

This book is copyright and reproduction of the whole or part without the publisher's written permission is prohibited.

First published 2002

08
10, 9, 8, 7, 6, 5, 4, 3

ISBN 978 0 435206 66 6

Illustrated by Andy Cooke
Cover illustration by Dave Cockburn
Cover Design by Paul Goodman
Designed by bigtop, Bicester, UK
Printed and bound in China through Phoenix Offset

Contents

MEASURES, SHAPE AND SPACE

Measures

Shape and space

HANDLING DATA

Organising and interpreting data

Let's practise

1 Key these numbers into your calculator.
Write what is on the display.

   a Seventeen thousand four hundred and thirty-seven

   b Twenty-two thousand and twenty-four

   c Forty thousand three hundred

   d Seventy thousand and eighty-seven

   e One hundred thousand two hundred and sixteen

   f Five hundred and six thousand and thirty

   g One million six hundred and twenty-one thousand
   two hundred and seventeen

2 Write each number in words.

   a 35 264   **b** 46 017   **c** 50 081

   d 273 021   **e** 460 002   **f** 1 580 300

3 Use a calculator to change the numbers in 1 step.
Write what you did for each.

   a 32 567 to 38 567   **b** 52 364 to 52 164

   c 78 009 to 81 009   **d** 82 076 to 32 076

25 987 to 25 487

I subtracted 500

Let's investigate

4 **a** Use all 7 digits to investigate
making the largest and
smallest numbers.

| 5 | 8 | 1 | 3 | 9 | 2 | 4 |

   b Write the numbers in both figures and words.

? What if you used only the odd digits for the largest number
and the even digits for the smallest number?

Let's practise

> To multiply by 10 we move the digits 1 place to the left.

> To multiply by 100 we move the digits 2 places to the left.

1 Multiply each number by 10.

    a 652   **b** 4217   **c** 7086

2 Multiply each number by 100.

    a 806   **b** 5372   **c** 8800

3 Each bag holds 10 sweets.
Each box holds 100 sweets.
How many sweets in:

    a 356 bags   **b** 569 boxes

    c 3472 bags   **d** 5198 boxes?

> To divide by 10 we move the digits 1 place to the right.

> To divide by 100 we move the digits 2 places to the right.

4 Divide by 10.

    a 7600   **b** 9000   **c** 3010

5 Divide by 100.

    a 4300   **b** 6000   **c** 8000

Let's investigate

6 **a** Copy and complete the chain.

b Investigate using different starting numbers and different starting boxes.

? What if you reversed the direction of the arrows and worked anticlockwise?

Let's practise

1 Copy and write **<** or **>** to make each statement correct.

a 32 560 ⬤ 32 650

b 372 002 ⬤ 371 998

c 426 780 ⬤ 462 870

d 606 060 ⬤ 600 606

2 Which alien in each pair has travelled further ?

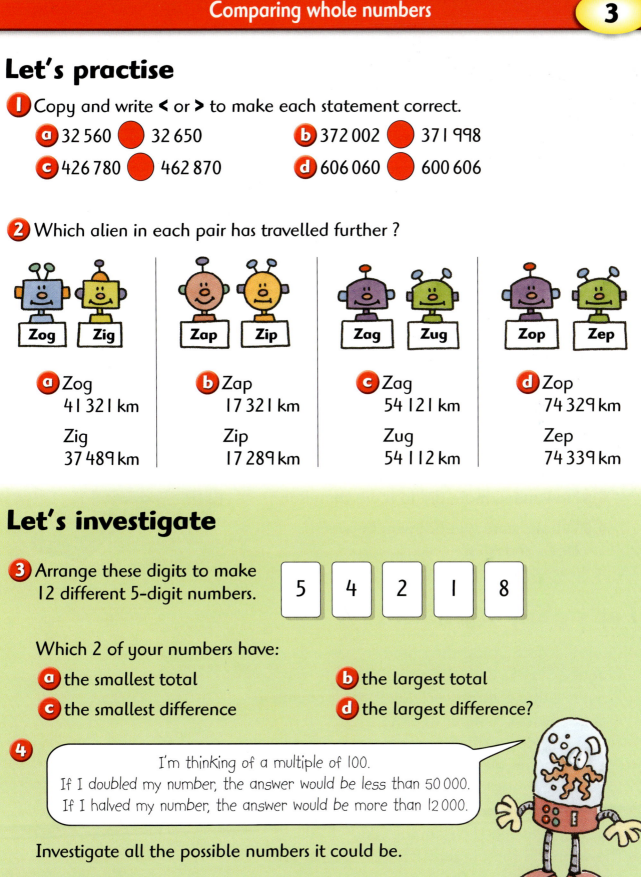

a Zog
41 321 km

Zig
37 489 km

b Zap
17 321 km

Zip
17 289 km

c Zag
54 121 km

Zug
54 112 km

d Zop
74 329 km

Zep
74 339 km

Let's investigate

3 Arrange these digits to make 12 different 5-digit numbers.

| 5 | 4 | 2 | 1 | 8 |

Which 2 of your numbers have:

a the smallest total

b the largest total

c the smallest difference

d the largest difference?

4
> I'm thinking of a multiple of 100.
> If I doubled my number, the answer would be less than 50 000.
> If I halved my number, the answer would be more than 12 000.

Investigate all the possible numbers it could be.

? What if:
when halved, the answer was less than 7000 and, when doubled, the answer was more than 17 000?

Let's practise

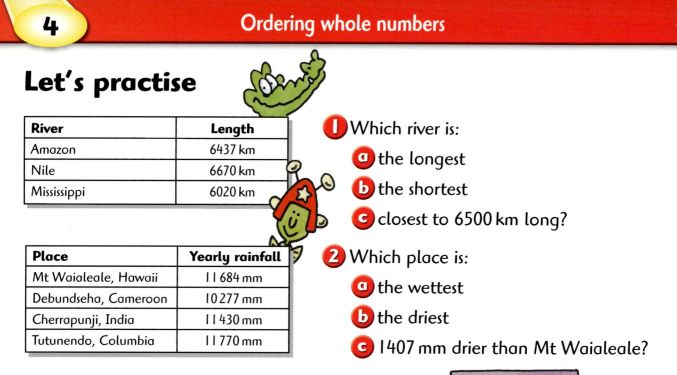

River	Length
Amazon	6437 km
Nile	6670 km
Mississippi	6020 km

1 Which river is:

a the longest

b the shortest

c closest to 6500 km long?

Place	Yearly rainfall
Mt Waialeale, Hawaii	11 684 mm
Debundseha, Cameroon	10 277 mm
Cherrapunji, India	11 430 mm
Tutunendo, Columbia	11 770 mm

2 Which place is:

a the wettest

b the driest

c 1407 mm drier than Mt Waialeale?

3 Some friends are playing a computer game.

a Who scored most?

b Who scored least?

c Who had the second highest score?

d How many more did Jo score than Rob?

e Whose score was halfway between Dev's and Ali's?

Jo　43 752

Dev　41 252

Rob　38 252

Ali　35 252

Crocodile in Denial!

Let's play　A game for 3

- Players 1 and 2 play the game.
  Player 3 checks with the calculator.
- Players 1 and 2 turn over 5 digit cards each and
  make a 5-digit number as close to 50 000 as possible.
- They write down the 2 numbers.
- Player 3 works out which player's number is nearer
  to 50 000. That player earns a point.
- Players earn an extra point if they can say a number
  that lies between their number and 50 000.
- The winner is the player with more points after
  6 rounds.

Swap roles.

You need

2 sets of digit cards
0 to 9

Let's practise

1 Estimate the distance travelled by each space shuttle.

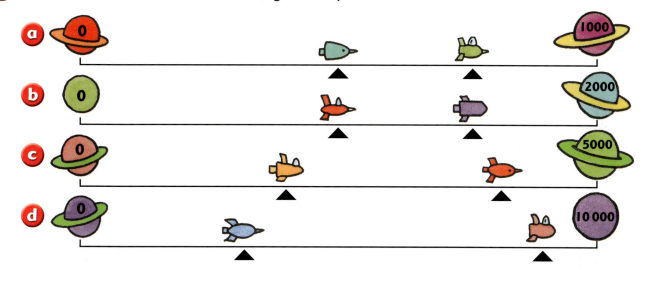

2 Estimate:

a How many 1p coins would make a line 1 m long?

b How many playing cards would cover your table?

c How many doors could fit side by side along the wall?

d How many times does your heart beat:
- in a minute   ● in an hour   ● in a day?

e Compare your estimates with those of a partner.

f How did you make your estimates?

Let's play   A game for 2

You need

a thick book, a bookmark or small piece of paper

Find how many pages are in the book.

- Slip the bookmark between 2 pages of the book without looking at the page number. Close the book.
  Each estimate the page number.
  The player who is closer scores a point.

- A player scores 3 extra points if they are exactly right.

The winner is the first player to score 10 or more points.

Let's practise

1 Estimate how far each rocket has travelled.

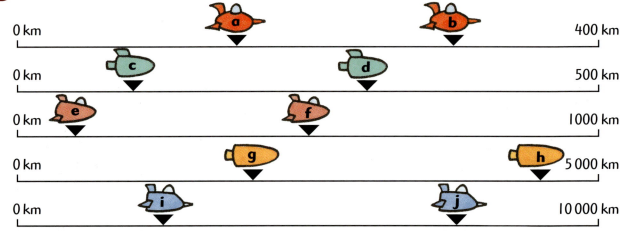

Let's solve problems

2 Estimate what fraction of each tube is filled.

Let's play A game for 2

You need
a ruler

- Draw a 10 cm line on a piece of paper.
  Label the ends 0 and 100.
- Each player writes 10 secret numbers between 0 and 100.
- Player 1 shows where their first number is on the number line, using a pencil as a pointer.
- Player 2 estimates what the number is. If Player 2 estimates the number within 10 either side then they earn a point.
- Swap roles.

The winner is the first to score 5 points.

? What happens if you change 100 to 1000 in the game?

Let's practise

1 Round the number of people in the space stations to the nearest 10.

a **2476**
b **6243**
c **8655**
d **9104**
e **7098**
f **8004**

2 Round the number of miles these asteroids have travelled to the nearest 100.

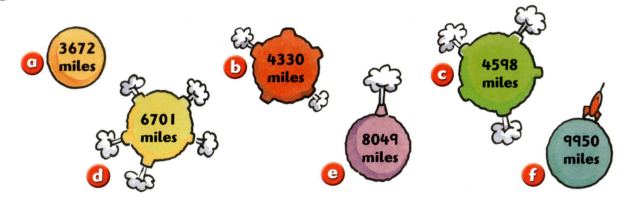

a **3672 miles**
b **4330 miles**
c **4598 miles**
d **6701 miles**
e **8049 miles**
f **9950 miles**

Let's play   A game for 2

You need

digit cards 0 to 9

Each player lists the first 10 multiples of 1000.

● Put the cards face down and take turns to choose 4 digit cards.

● Make a number.

6 2 0 3

● Round the number to the nearest 1000.
6203 → 6000

● Cross off the number on your list. ~~6000~~

The winner is the first player to cross off all their numbers.

Let's practise

1 Copy the sequences, writing 3 more numbers for each.

a 5, 4, 3, 2, ...

b 8, 6, 4, 2, ...

c 15, 10, 5, 0, ...

d 6, 3, 0, –3, ...

e –9, –7, –5, –3, ...

f –2, –5, –8, –11, ...

2 Write the numbers in order, lowest first.

a 4 –3 1

b –3 3 –6

c –10 –20 8 0

d –17 –18 –19 16

e –12 0 –4 –7

f –9 –6 –7 –11

Let's play   A game for 2

You need a counter, a dice

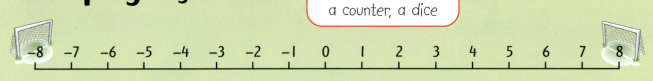

- Put the counter on 0.
- Take turns to roll the dice.
- Player 1 moves the counter to the right and Player 2 moves it to the left, to match the number on the dice.
- Replace the counter on 0 after a goal.

The winner is the first to score 3 goals.

Let's investigate

3 **a** Copy these cards. Write numbers on the blank cards so that the 7 numbers are in order.

b Do this as many ways as you can.

Let's practise

1 **a** What temperature does the thermometer show?

b What will be the temperature if it becomes 8 °C warmer?

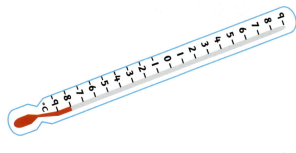

2 What will be the temperature if it is:

a −5 °C and rises by 15 °C

b 26 °C and falls by 31 °C

c −8 °C and rises by 15 °C, then falls by 9 °C

d 30 °C and falls by 45 °C, then rises by 17 °C?

3 The temperature is:

a 13 °C. It falls to −26 °C. How many degrees has it fallen?

b −19 °C. It rises to 5 °C. How many degrees has it risen?

c 21 °C. How many degrees must it fall to reach −9 °C?

d −4 °C. How many degrees must it rise to reach 18 °C?

Let's play A game for 1

You need

a set of playing cards with the picture cards removed

Start with a 'total' of 0.

● Put the cards in a pile, face down.

● Turn over one at a time.
  If it is a red card, count **back** that number from your total.
  If it is a black card, count **on** that number from your total.

● How many cards does it take to reach either 15 or −15?

Play again and try to beat your record.

Let's practise

1 Copy and complete each sequence.

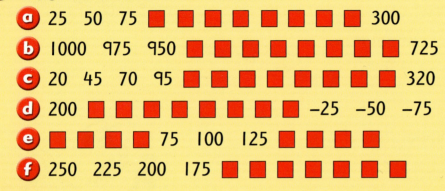

a 25 50 75 ■ ■ ■ ■ ■ ■ ■ 300

b 1000 975 950 ■ ■ ■ ■ ■ ■ ■ 725

c 20 45 70 95 ■ ■ ■ ■ ■ ■ ■ 320

d 200 ■ ■ ■ ■ ■ ■ ■ ■ –25 –50 –75

e ■ ■ ■ ■ 75 100 125 ■ ■ ■ ■

f 250 225 200 175 ■ ■ ■ ■ ■ ■ ■

2 **a** Copy this number line.

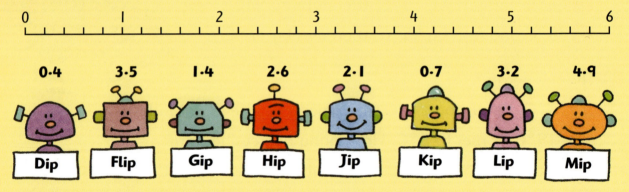

0   1   2   3   4   5   6

0·4	3·5	1·4	2·6	2·1	0·7	3·2	4·9
Dip	Flip	Gip	Hip	Jip	Kip	Lip	Mip

b Mark with a cross where each robot should stand. Label it with the robot's name.

c Each robot takes 4 steps of 0·2 along the line. Mark each robot's new position.

Let's play A game for 2

- Take turns to choose a robot number from question 2.
- Player 1 counts forward aloud in steps of 0·3.
- Player 2 checks using the calculator.
- Stop when the number is greater than 7.
  Players earn 1 point for each correct count.
- Swap roles.

The winner is the player with more points after 5 turns each.

? What if you counted back in steps of 0·3 and stopped when the number was less than –5?

Let's practise

1 Find 5 pairs from the numbers that give an odd total.
Write the total for each pair.

142　67

422　291

190　184　391　263

Let's investigate

2

1	2	3	4	5	6	7	8	9	10
11	12	13	14	15	16	17	18	19	20
21	22	23	24	25	26	27	28	29	30
31	32	33	34	35	36	37	38	39	40
41	42	43	44	45	46	47	48	49	50
51	52	53	54	55	56	57	58	59	60
61	62	63	64	65	66	67	68	69	70
71	72	73	74	75	76	77	78	79	80
81	82	83	84	85	86	87	88	89	90
91	92	93	94	95	96	97	98	99	100

You need

15 small counters

- Choose a number on the square less than 50.
  Add it to one of the numbers either side.
- Record your addition and put a counter on the answer on the number square.
  Example: Choose 23, add it to 24, put a counter on 47.
- Do this 15 times.
- What do you notice about the numbers either side of the counters?
- What does this tell you about the numbers that are covered up?

Let's practise

1 Write the numbers that are divisible by 2.

2857

761

241

2004

846

262

1358

1 000 000

895

Let's investigate 📱

2 If a number is divisible by 4, the last 2 digits of the number are divisible by 4.

Use halving and halving again to see if a number is divisible by 4

152

If the last digit is even, halve the last 2 digits.

52
26   26

If the answer is even halve it again.

26
13   13

The number 152 is divisible by 4.

13 x 4 = 52

a Why do you think the hundreds digit can be ignored? Explain.

b Investigate these numbers to see whether they are divisible by 4.

264

154

146

416

334

172

c Use a calculator to check.

Let's practise

1 Complete the multiplications. Make each pair of factors different.

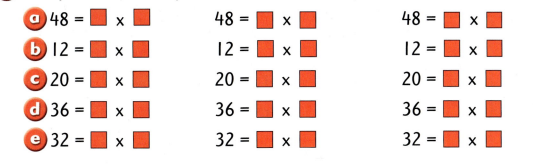

a) 48 = ☐ x ☐   48 = ☐ x ☐   48 = ☐ x ☐

b) 12 = ☐ x ☐   12 = ☐ x ☐   12 = ☐ x ☐

c) 20 = ☐ x ☐   20 = ☐ x ☐   20 = ☐ x ☐

d) 36 = ☐ x ☐   36 = ☐ x ☐   36 = ☐ x ☐

e) 32 = ☐ x ☐   32 = ☐ x ☐   32 = ☐ x ☐

Let's play   A game for 2

You need
40 interlocking cubes, number cards 1–20, 2 dice

- Each turn over a number card.
- Take the number of cubes shown on your card.
- Score 1 point for each different rectangle you can make.
- Score 2 points if you can make a square.
- Each rectangle or square must use all the cubes.

Remember that a square is a rectangle.

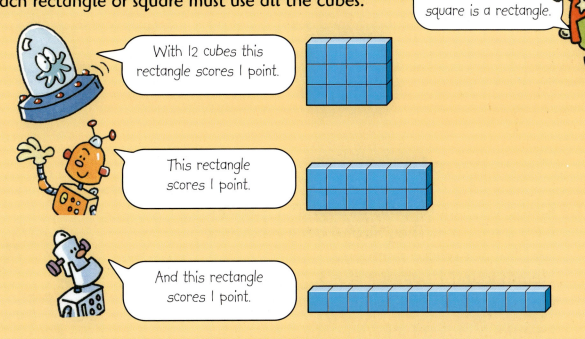

With 12 cubes this rectangle scores 1 point.

This rectangle scores 1 point.

And this rectangle scores 1 point.

- After 5 rounds who has scored more points?

Find a way to record the factors.

? What if you rolled 2 dice to make a 2-digit number?
Record the number and its factors.

Let's practise

1 **a** Copy and complete.

Numerator	Denominator	Fraction
3	5	
	9	$\frac{2}{9}$
5		$\frac{5}{8}$
6	5	
	3	$\frac{5}{3}$
13		$\frac{13}{4}$

b Compare the first 3 fractions with the last 3.
What do you notice about the fractions?

2 Copy and complete.

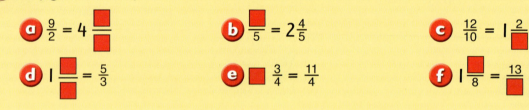

a $\frac{9}{2} = 4\frac{\square}{\square}$

b $\frac{\square}{5} = 2\frac{4}{5}$

c $\frac{12}{10} = 1\frac{2}{\square}$

d $1\frac{\square}{\square} = \frac{5}{3}$

e $\square\frac{3}{4} = \frac{11}{4}$

f $1\frac{\square}{8} = \frac{13}{\square}$

Let's investigate

3 **a** Khalid investigates pairs of improper fractions
with a sum of 3. They have a denominator of 3
and are not whole numbers.
He has found 1 pair: $\frac{4}{3} + \frac{5}{3} = 3$.
Find other pairs for Khalid.

b Investigate pairs of improper fractions.
They must have a denominator of 3 and a sum of 4, 5, 6 or 7.

? What if the pairs of fractions each had a denominator of 4?

Let's practise

1 Copy and complete.

a $\frac{3}{8} + \frac{5}{8} = \blacksquare$

b $\frac{4}{10} + \frac{\blacksquare}{\blacksquare} = 1$

c $\frac{2}{\blacksquare} + \frac{3}{\blacksquare} = 1$

2 Copy and write **<**, **>** or **=** to make each statement correct.

a $\frac{3}{8}$ ◯ $\frac{1}{2}$

b $\frac{4}{10}$ ◯ $\frac{1}{2}$

c $\frac{5}{6}$ ◯ $\frac{1}{2}$

d $\frac{3}{5}$ ◯ $\frac{1}{2}$

e $\frac{2}{5}$ ◯ $\frac{1}{2}$

f $\frac{50}{100}$ ◯ $\frac{1}{2}$

g $\frac{3}{6}$ ◯ $\frac{1}{2}$

h $\frac{5}{8}$ ◯ $\frac{1}{2}$

i $\frac{40}{100}$ ◯ $\frac{1}{2}$

3 Copy and write 4 more equivalent fractions in each pattern.

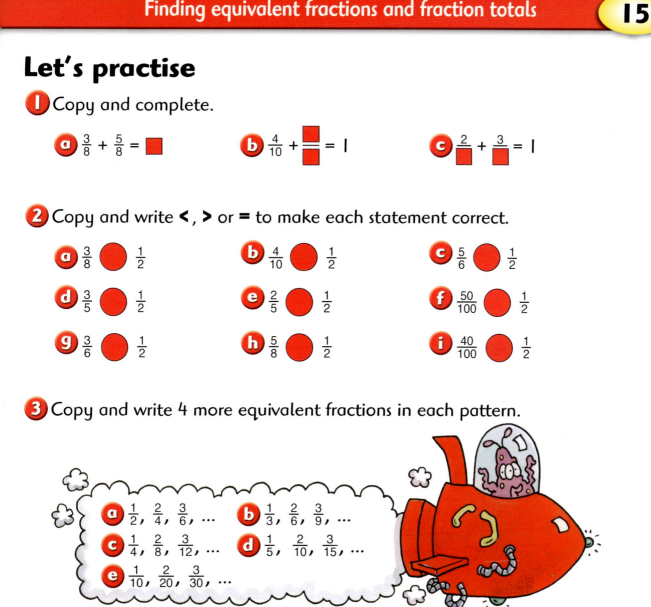

a $\frac{1}{2}, \frac{2}{4}, \frac{3}{6}, \ldots$ **b** $\frac{1}{3}, \frac{2}{6}, \frac{3}{9}, \ldots$

c $\frac{1}{4}, \frac{2}{8}, \frac{3}{12}, \ldots$ **d** $\frac{1}{5}, \frac{2}{10}, \frac{3}{15}, \ldots$

e $\frac{1}{10}, \frac{2}{20}, \frac{3}{30}, \ldots$

Write about how the numerators and denominators in each pattern change.

Let's investigate

You need

a dice

4 • Roll the dice twice to make a fraction: the first number is the numerator, the second the denominator. Record the fractions.

$\frac{3}{5}$

• Do this 20 times.
• Investigate the set of 20 fractions and record:
   ◆ the fractions less than 1, equal to 1 and greater than 1
   ◆ sets of equivalent fractions.

Let's practise

1 Copy and complete.

a $\frac{1}{4}$ of 12 = ▨   **b** $\frac{1}{3}$ of 36 = ▨   **c** $\frac{1}{5}$ of 25 = ▨   **d** $\frac{1}{100}$ of 100 = ▨

Write about how you worked out the answers.

2 Copy and complete.

a $\frac{3}{4}$ of 12 = ▨   **b** $\frac{2}{3}$ of 36 = ▨   **c** $\frac{4}{5}$ of 25 = ▨   **d** $\frac{7}{100}$ of 100 = ▨

Write about how you worked out the answers.

Let's solve problems

$\frac{15}{3}$ is another way of writing 15 ÷ 3

3 Write these in another way and find each answer.

a $\frac{16}{4}$ **b** 21 ÷ 7   **c** $\frac{18}{6}$ **d** 13 ÷ 2

4 The Kitchen Robots haven't made the right amount of food. If they share the food equally, how much can each alien have?

a 3 mud cakes between 7 Flobsters.

b 2 fruit flings between 6 Glibs.

c 6 pumice pizzas between 3 Thralls.

d 7 cheese ships between 4 Silicas.

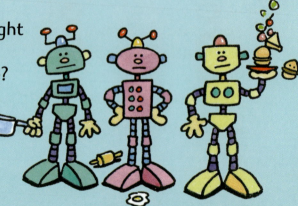

5 Write a word problem and give the solution for:

a $\frac{12}{3}$ **b** $\frac{15}{4}$

Let's solve problems

The inhabitants of Planet Zebron make drinks with these juices.

lime · cherry · orange · lemon · kiwi · strawberry · coconut

1 Gargol makes a 60 ml drink with 1 part lime and 2 parts cherry.

a How much lime does he use?

b What proportion of the drink is cherry?

2 Aux makes a cocktail with 40 ml of coconut and 10 ml of lemon juice.

a How many millilitres are in the drink?

b For every 5 ml of lemon juice how many ml of coconut juice are there?

c What is the proportion of lemon in the drink?

3 Zang makes a 90 ml drink. One half of it is kiwi juice.
The other half is 2 parts strawberry for every 1 part orange.
How many millilitres of each juice are in the drink?

Let's investigate

lime	cherry	orange	lemon	kiwi	strawberry	coconut
10 ml	15 ml	20 ml	25 ml	10 ml	15 ml	20 ml

4 Blip made a 50 ml drink with 3 whole bottles of juice.

a Which 3 juices could he have used?

b What was the proportion of each juice in the drink?

c Investigate making different 50 ml drinks with 3 whole bottles of juice.
Write the proportion of each juice used in the drinks.

? What if 4 whole bottles were used for a 50 ml drink?

Let's practise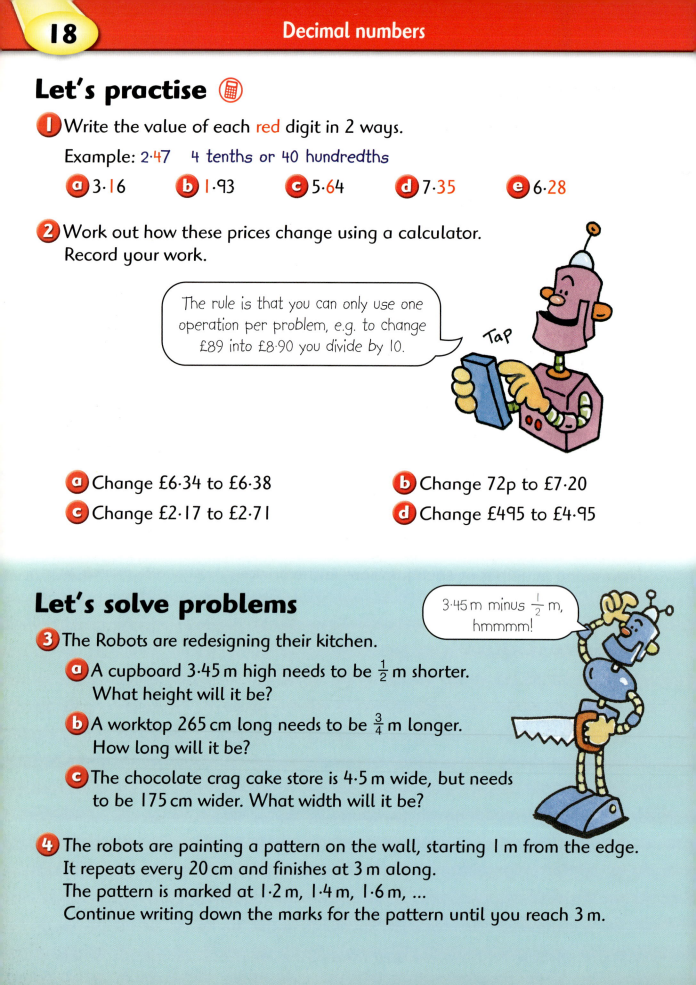

1 Write the value of each red digit in 2 ways.

Example: 2·47   4 tenths or 40 hundredths

a 3·16   **b** 1·93   **c** 5·64   **d** 7·35   **e** 6·28

2 Work out how these prices change using a calculator.
Record your work.

> The rule is that you can only use one operation per problem, e.g. to change £89 into £8·90 you divide by 10.

Tap

a Change £6·34 to £6·38

b Change 72p to £7·20

c Change £2·17 to £2·71

d Change £495 to £4·95

Let's solve problems

> 3·45 m minus ½ m, hmmmm!

3 The Robots are redesigning their kitchen.

a A cupboard 3·45 m high needs to be ½ m shorter. What height will it be?

b A worktop 265 cm long needs to be ¾ m longer. How long will it be?

c The chocolate crag cake store is 4·5 m wide, but needs to be 175 cm wider. What width will it be?

4 The robots are painting a pattern on the wall, starting 1 m from the edge. It repeats every 20 cm and finishes at 3 m along. The pattern is marked at 1·2 m, 1·4 m, 1·6 m, ... Continue writing down the marks for the pattern until you reach 3 m.

Let's practise

1 Round to the nearest whole number.

a 3·6 **b** 8·4 **c** 13·2 **d** 15·7 **e** 12·5

2 Round to the nearest metre.

a 2·4 m **b** 16·8 m **c** 7·5 m **d** 3·68 m **e** 8·19 m

3 Round to the nearest £.

a £1·25 **b** £2·09 **c** £1·76 **d** £25·51 **e** £17·85

4 Copy and write the equivalent decimal fractions.

a $\frac{2}{100}$ **b** $\frac{41}{100}$ **c** $\frac{17}{100}$ **d** $\frac{9}{100}$ **e** $\frac{3}{4}$

Let's investigate

5 Remember that $\frac{1}{4}$ is another way of writing $1 \div 4$.
We can use this to find equivalent decimal fractions using the calculator.

Example: $\boxed{1} \boxed{\div} \boxed{4} \boxed{=} \boxed{0·25}$

a Investigate what happens when you convert fraction families into decimal fractions. Record your work carefully.

• quarters • thirds • fifths • sixths • eighths • tenths

b What happens if you continue the families into improper fractions?

Fraction	$\frac{1}{4}$,	$\frac{2}{4}$,	$\frac{3}{4}$,	$\frac{4}{4}$,	$\frac{5}{4}$, ...
Decimal	0·25,	0·5, ...			

c Write about the patterns you notice.

Let's practise

1 Copy and complete. $\dfrac{10}{100} = 10\%$

a $\dfrac{20}{100} = \blacksquare\%$

b $\dfrac{\blacksquare}{100} = 30\%$

c $\dfrac{50}{\blacksquare} = 50\%$

d $\dfrac{25}{\blacksquare} = 25\%$

e $\dfrac{\blacksquare}{\blacksquare} = 75\%$

f $\dfrac{\blacksquare}{\blacksquare} = 5\%$

2 Any 'hundredth' can be a percentage. Other fractions can be percentages, too.

Example: $\dfrac{10}{100} = \dfrac{1}{10} = 10\%$

Copy and complete.

a $\dfrac{20}{100} = \dfrac{\blacksquare}{10} = \blacksquare\%$

b $50\% = \dfrac{\blacksquare}{100} = \dfrac{\blacksquare}{10}$

c $\dfrac{40}{100} = \dfrac{\blacksquare}{\blacksquare} = \blacksquare\%$

d $\dfrac{70}{100} = \dfrac{7}{10} = \blacksquare\%$

e $\dfrac{\blacksquare}{100} = \dfrac{3}{10} = \blacksquare\%$

f $\dfrac{60}{100} = \dfrac{\blacksquare}{\blacksquare} = \blacksquare\%$

Let's solve problems

3 The Murgs need to paint their space station. They have 8 colours to choose from, but only enough of each to paint the fraction shown below:

yellow	$\dfrac{1}{4}$	purple	$\dfrac{5}{100}$
blue	$\dfrac{1}{2}$	orange	$\dfrac{15}{100}$
red	$\dfrac{3}{4}$	pink	$\dfrac{4}{10}$
green	$\dfrac{3}{10}$	silver	$\dfrac{1}{10}$

Convert the fractions into percentages. The colours must add to 100%.

They look for different ways of painting the space station.

Example: orange $\dfrac{15}{100}$ or 15%

         silver $\dfrac{1}{10}$ or 10%

         red $\dfrac{3}{4}$ or 75%

a Find another way that uses just 3 colours.

b Which way uses: • fewest colours   • most colours?

? What if the Murgs used exactly 4 colours? How many ways are there of doing this?

Let's practise

1 Copy and complete. $\frac{1}{2}$ = 0.5 = 50%

a $\frac{1}{10}$ = 0·1 = ☐ %

b $\frac{1}{4}$ = ☐·☐ ☐ = 25%

c $\frac{1}{5}$ = 0·2 = ☐ %

d $\frac{☐}{☐}$ = 0.4 = ☐ %

e $\frac{3}{4}$ = ☐·☐ ☐ = 75%

f $\frac{☐}{☐}$ = ☐·☐ = 90%

Let's play A game for 1

Game 1

- You need the number 1 card and the decimal and percentage cards.
- Shuffle the cards and place them face down in 2 rows of 7.
- Turn over 2 cards.
- If they are equivalent, leave them face up; if not, turn them both back over and choose another 2 cards.
- Continue until you have found all the pairs.

> **You need**
> a set of cards from Activity Sheet 15

Game 2

- The rules are the same as for Game 1.

> **You need**
> the number 1 card and the fraction and percentage cards

Let's investigate

2 Investigate changing hundredths into percentages.

- Predict what $\frac{1}{100}$ is as a percentage.
- Now use your calculator like this: ☐1☐ ☐÷☐ ☐1☐ ☐0☐ ☐0☐ ☐%☐
- Write the number you see on the display.
- Do the same for other numbers of hundredths. Give at least 5 examples.
- Write about the patterns you notice.

? What if you used tenths instead of hundredths? ☐1☐ ☐÷☐ ☐1☐ ☐0☐ ☐%☐

Let's practise

1 Copy and complete.

a $10\% = \frac{\square}{100}$ **b** $\square\% = \frac{50}{100}$ **c** $25\% = \frac{1}{\square}$

d $\square\% = \frac{2}{5}$ **e** $\square\% = \frac{3}{4}$ **f** $20\% = \frac{1}{\square}$

2 Work out these percentages.

a 25% of 10 kg   **b** 40% of 10 kg   **c** 25% of £6

d 50% of 12 m   **e** 75% of £16   **f** 20% of 20 m

Let's solve problems

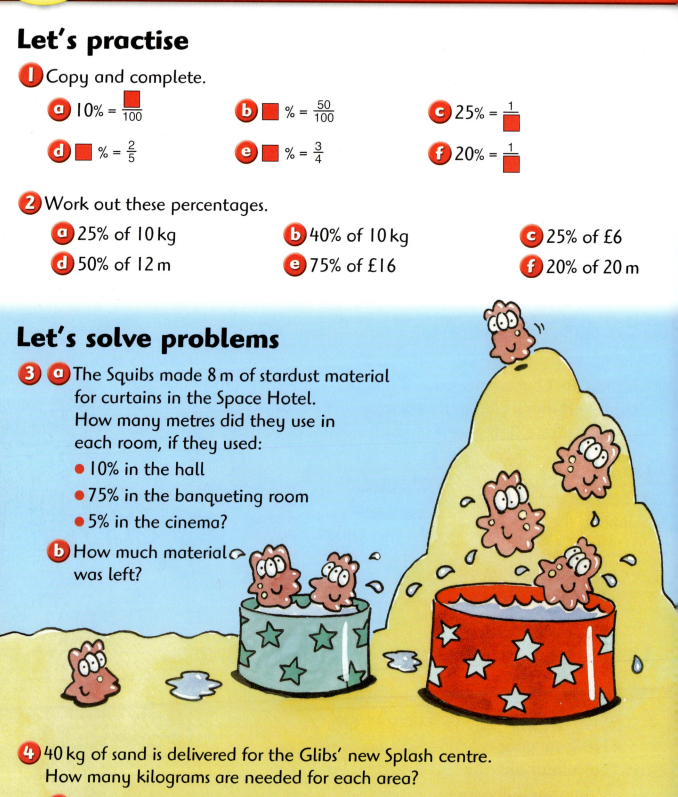

3 **a** The Squibs made 8 m of stardust material for curtains in the Space Hotel. How many metres did they use in each room, if they used:

● 10% in the hall

● 75% in the banqueting room

● 5% in the cinema?

b How much material was left?

4 40 kg of sand is delivered for the Glibs' new Splash centre. How many kilograms are needed for each area?

a 20% is for the baby Glib pool

b 50% is for the toddler Glib pool

c 30% is for the small Glib beach.

d Is there any sand left?

Let's practise

1 Start each calculation with 5734.

a subtract 100   **b** plus 80   **c** minus 70   **d** add 400

e subtract 600   **f** decrease by 900   **g** increase by 500   **h** take 800

Let's investigate

2 This addition has 5 different digits.

3 7 + 8 = 4 5

Investigate making other additions and subtractions using 5 different digits.

Remember... the calculations must have a correct answer.

3 Jacqui's telephone number is 625439.
She separates the digits.

62 / 54 / 39
That could be 62 + 54 + 39 which has a total of 155.

Find the totals when the same digits are separated like this:

a 6 / 25 / 43 / 9

b 625 / 439

c 6 / 2 / 5 / 43 / 9

d 62 / 5 / 4 / 39

Investigate separating the digits in other ways. Find the total each time.

What if the phone number was 791846?

Let's practise

1 Start each calculation with 678.

a subtract 35   **b** plus 30   **c** decrease by 90   **d** add 128

e take 18   **f** increase by 306   **g** plus 210   **h** minus 99

2 Write 2 additions and 2 subtractions using the numbers on the planets.

217 + 142 = 359

3 Use sets of 3 numbers from the landing craft to write as many additions and subtractions as you can.

564 − 215 = 349

Let's investigate

4 Investigate making pairs of 3-digit numbers using the digits on the blocks. Find their difference. Which pairs have the smallest and the greatest differences?

612 954

$$954$$
$$-612$$
difference = 342

Let's practise

1 These space power packs can hold 1 litre of fuel each.
The numbers show how much fuel is left.
How much more fuel is needed to fill each pack?

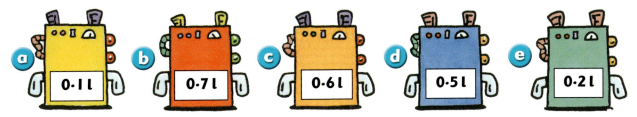

a **0·1 l**   b **0·7 l**   c **0·6 l**   d **0·5 l**   e **0·2 l**

Let's play   A game for 2

Shuffle the digit cards and place them, face down,
in 5 rows of 4.

You need
2 sets of 0 to 9
digit cards,
2 decimal point cards

- Take turns to turn over 4 cards.
- Try to arrange them to make 2
  decimal numbers that total 10.
- Record if the addition makes 10.
- If not, replace the cards face down.
- Score a point each time you make 10.

The winner is the first player to score 6 points.

| 6 | · | 4 | 3 | · | 6 |

That is 6·4 + 3·6 = 10.
I score 1 point.

Let's investigate

2 Investigate different ways of completing this addition
using any 4 digits. You may not use a digit more than once.

☐ · ☐ + ☐ · ☐ = 10   2·1 + 7·9 = 10

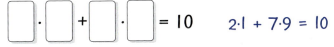

a Record each addition.

b Sort and then order the additions according to the units digit
of the first numbers.

? What if the sum of the 2 decimal numbers was 9, 8, 7 ..., 1?

Let's practise

1 **a** 68 + 32 = ☐   **b** 19 + 81 = ☐   **c** 27 + 73 = ☐

   d 44 + ☐ = 100   **e** 65 + ☐ = 100   **f** ☐ + 38 = 100

2 Copy the grid. Arrange the star numbers in the grid so that each row and column adds up to 1000.

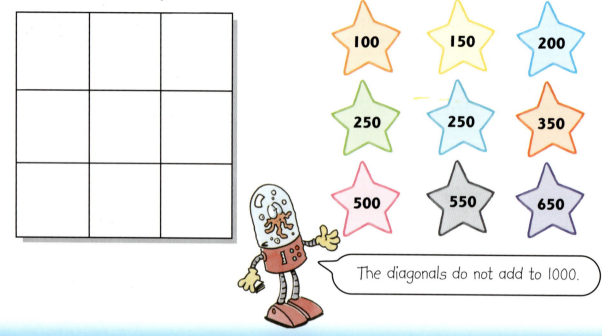

100   150   200

250   250   350

500   550   650

The diagonals do not add to 1000.

Let's play   A game for 2

You need

2 sets of 0 to 9 digit cards

Shuffle the cards and place them, face down, in 5 rows of 4.
● Take turns to turn over 4 cards.
● Try to arrange them to make 2 numbers that total 100.
● Record if the addition makes 100.

3   2   6   8

32 + 68 = 100

● If not, replace the cards, face down.
● Score a point each time you make 100.
The winner is the first player to score 6 points.

Let's practise

1 How many years ago was:

a 1996   **b** 1987   **c** 1979   **d** 1998   **e** 1989   **f** 1968?

2 Jack is travelling forwards and backwards in his time machine.
He starts in the year 2996 and his first journey is forward to 8006.

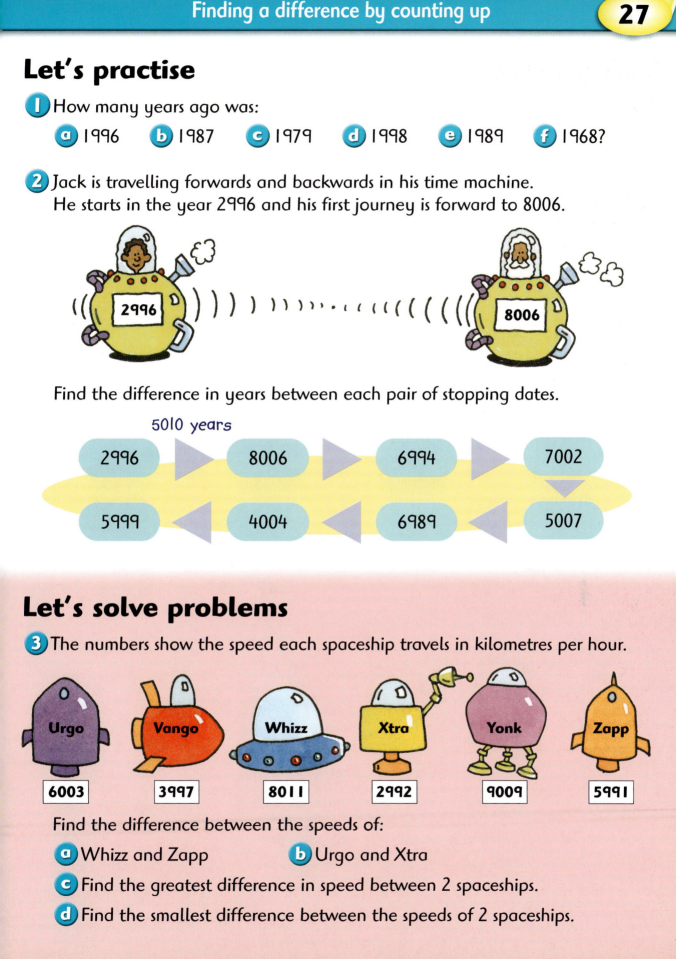

Find the difference in years between each pair of stopping dates.

5010 years

2996	▶	8006	▶	6994	▶	7002

5999	◀	4004	◀	6989	◀	5007

Let's solve problems

3 The numbers show the speed each spaceship travels in kilometres per hour.

Urgo **6003**   Vango **3997**   Whizz **8011**   Xtra **2992**   Yonk **9009**   Zapp **5991**

Find the difference between the speeds of:

a Whizz and Zapp   **b** Urgo and Xtra

c Find the greatest difference in speed between 2 spaceships.

d Find the smallest difference between the speeds of 2 spaceships.

Let's practise

Here is a way of finding
the answer to 125 + 28.

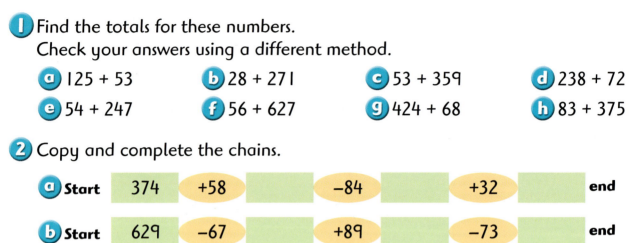

1	2	0	+	2	0	=	1	4	0
		5	+		8	=		1	3
1	4	0	+	1	3	=	1	5	3

1 Find the totals for these numbers.
Check your answers using a different method.

a 125 + 53   **b** 28 + 271   **c** 53 + 359   **d** 238 + 72

e 54 + 247   **f** 56 + 627   **g** 424 + 68   **h** 83 + 375

2 Copy and complete the chains.

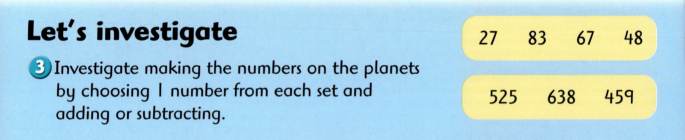

a Start   374   +58   −84   +32   end

b Start   629   −67   +89   −73   end

Let's investigate

3 Investigate making the numbers on the planets
by choosing 1 number from each set and
adding or subtracting.

| 27 | 83 | 67 | 48 |

| 525 | 638 | 459 |

Planet
Alva
442

Planet
Barto
507

Planet
Dauria
432

Planet
Chao
555

Planet
Eisinga
592

Let's practise

1 **a** double 1·6 = ☐　　**b** double 2·4 = ☐　　**c** double 3·7 = ☐

　　d double ☐ = 10·8　　**e** double ☐ = 13·4　　**f** double ☐ = 3·6

2 Copy the walls.

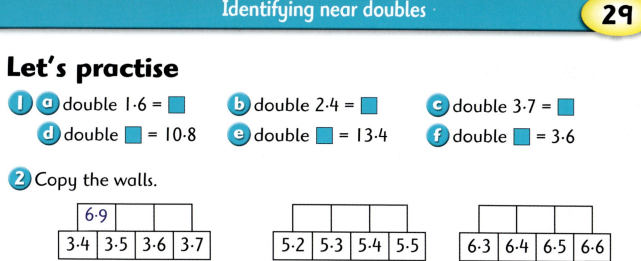

6·9		
3·4	3·5	3·6	3·7

5·2	5·3	5·4	5·5

6·3	6·4	6·5	6·6

a Write the total of the 2 touching numbers in the brick above.

b Write what you notice about the numbers in each top row.

3 1·5 1·6 1·7 1·8 1·9 2·0 2·1 2·2 2·3 2·4 2·5 2·6 2·7 2·8 2·9 3·0 3·1 3·2 3·3 3·4 3·5 3·6 3·7 3·8

Find these totals using 2 adjacent decimals from the number line. 1·6 + 1·7 = 3·3

a 3·5　　**b** 3·1　　**c** 5·1　　**d** 3·7　　**e** 6·3　　**f** 6·7　　**g** 7·1

Let's investigate

4 Investigate sums of 3 consecutive decimals on the number line in question 3.

? What if you investigated sums of 4 consecutive decimals
on the number line?
What about sums of 5 consecutive decimals?

Let's practise

1. (a) 438 + 61 = ☐   (b) 582 + 71 = ☐   (c) 637 + 81 = ☐

   (d) 438 − 61 = ☐   (e) 582 − 71 = ☐   (f) 637 − 81 = ☐

2. Copy and complete the chain.

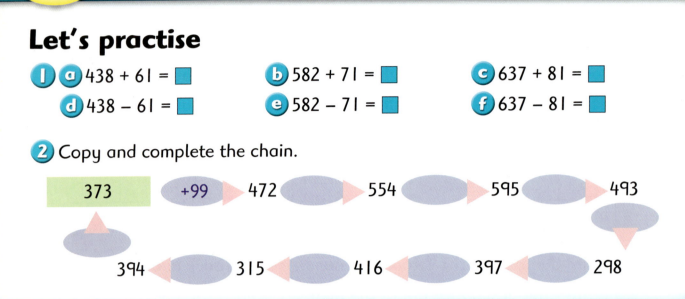

373   +99 ▶ 472 ▶ 554 ▶ 595 ▶ 493

394 ◀ 315 ◀ 416 ◀ 397 ◀ 298

Let's play   A game for 2

- Choose numbers from the satellite pairs to make additions or subtractions. Make 10 questions.
- Swap questions with your partner.
- Answer your partner's questions, then swap back to check.

  258 + 99 = 357

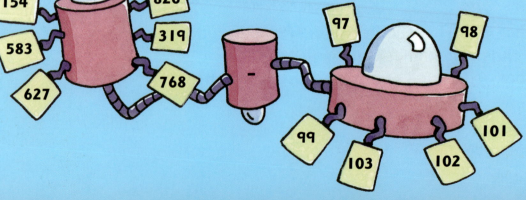

Let's practise

1 Write the totals of the numbers in each flying saucer.

> Check your answers by adding them in a different order.

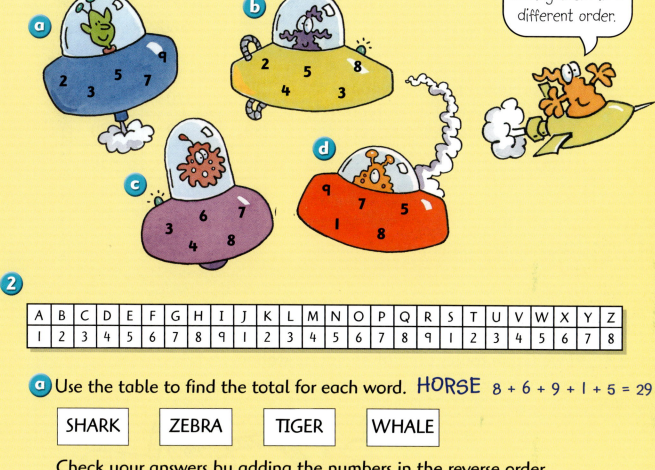

a 9 2 5 7 3

b 2 5 8 4 3

c 6 7 3 4 8

d 9 7 5 1 8

2

A	B	C	D	E	F	G	H	I	J	K	L	M	N	O	P	Q	R	S	T	U	V	W	X	Y	Z
1	2	3	4	5	6	7	8	9	1	2	3	4	5	6	7	8	9	1	2	3	4	5	6	7	8

a Use the table to find the total for each word. **HORSE** 8 + 6 + 9 + 1 + 5 = 29

SHARK	ZEBRA	TIGER	WHALE

Check your answers by adding the numbers in the reverse order.

b Find 3-letter creatures with a total of:

5   6   14   17

Let's investigate

3 Investigate different totals that can be made using 3 numbers from the satellite.

a What is the smallest possible total?

b What is the largest possible total?

? What if you used 4 numbers?

40 30
20
80 50
60
70

Let's practise

1 Add 600 to each number.

a 24   **b** 379   **c** 627   **d** 888

e 734   **f** 495   **g** 931   **h** 560

2 a Add or subtract a pair of numbers from the grid that give an answer between 500 and 551.

$980 - 460 = 520$

230	370	910
280	460	720
890	110	430
360	470	980

b Repeat for 5 other pairs of numbers.

Let's investigate

3 a Investigate routes through the space station with a total of 1500. Record each addition.

b Investigate routes with other totals.

Let's practise

1 How much more is needed to fill each space pack?

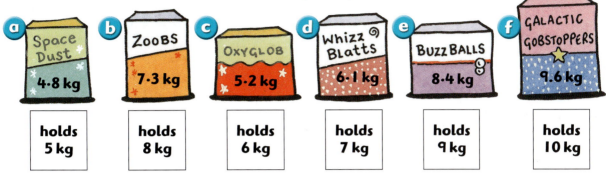

a Space Dust 4·8 kg — holds 5 kg

b ZOOBS 7·3 kg — holds 8 kg

c OXYGLOB 5·2 kg — holds 6 kg

d Whizz Blatts 6·1 kg — holds 7 kg

e BUZZ BALLS 8·4 kg — holds 9 kg

f GALACTIC GOBSTOPPERS 9·6 kg — holds 10 kg

Let's solve problems

2

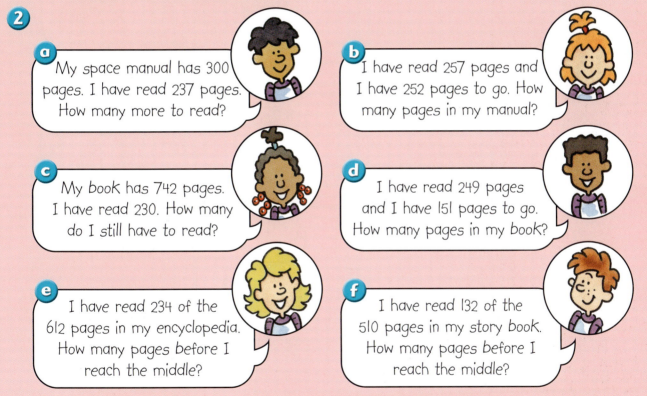

a My space manual has 300 pages. I have read 237 pages. How many more to read?

b I have read 257 pages and I have 252 pages to go. How many pages in my manual?

c My book has 742 pages. I have read 230. How many do I still have to read?

d I have read 249 pages and I have 151 pages to go. How many pages in my book?

e I have read 234 of the 612 pages in my encyclopedia. How many pages before I reach the middle?

f I have read 132 of the 510 pages in my story book. How many pages before I reach the middle?

3 In our space school there are 415 trainee astronauts.
How many trainees did not have school dinners on each of the days?

Trainees having school dinners				
Monday	Tuesday	Wednesday	Thursday	Friday
226	195	187	242	338

Let's practise

Check your answers using subtraction.

1 Copy and complete.

a   587
   + 475

b   628
   + 594

c   8754
   + 675

d   6387
   + 859

2 **a** 719 plus 482

b Add 964 and 308

c The total of 3054 and 656

d The sum of 5207 and 836

Let's investigate

3 Dib has added pairs of numbers and written the answers in a grid. The answers go horizontally and vertically.

3742 + 873

5247 + 695

3518 + 5329

2597 + 1406

1275 + 3309

3529 + 3451

1089 + 351

2385 + 2888

4	5	8	3
6	8	8	0
1	4	3	0
5	1	7	6

Five of the digits in the grid are incorrect. Draw the grid with the correct answers.

Let's practise

1 Copy and complete.

a
```
    ☐ 5 4
  + 6 8 8
    9 4 ☐
```

b
```
    7 ☐ 3
  + ☐ 3 7
    8 9 ☐
```

c
```
    6 ☐ 9
  + 2 5 ☐
    ☐ 0 4
```

Check your answers using subtraction.

d
```
    ☐ 4 7
  + 3 6 ☐
    9 ☐ 6
```

e
```
      9 ☐ 4
  +   2 7 ☐
    ☐ 2 5 8
```

f
```
      6 ☐ 1
  +   ☐ 4 8
    ☐ 1 6 9
```

g
```
    ☐ 2 9
  + 4 ☐ ☐
    8 6 2
```

Let's investigate

2 **a** Write a 3-digit number using 3 consecutive digits. Reverse the digits and find the sum of the 2 numbers. Find all the different ways of doing this.

```
    1 2 3
  + 3 2 1
    4 4 4
```

b Write about any patterns you notice in the answers.

? What if you used 3 consecutive even digits or 3 consecutive odd digits?

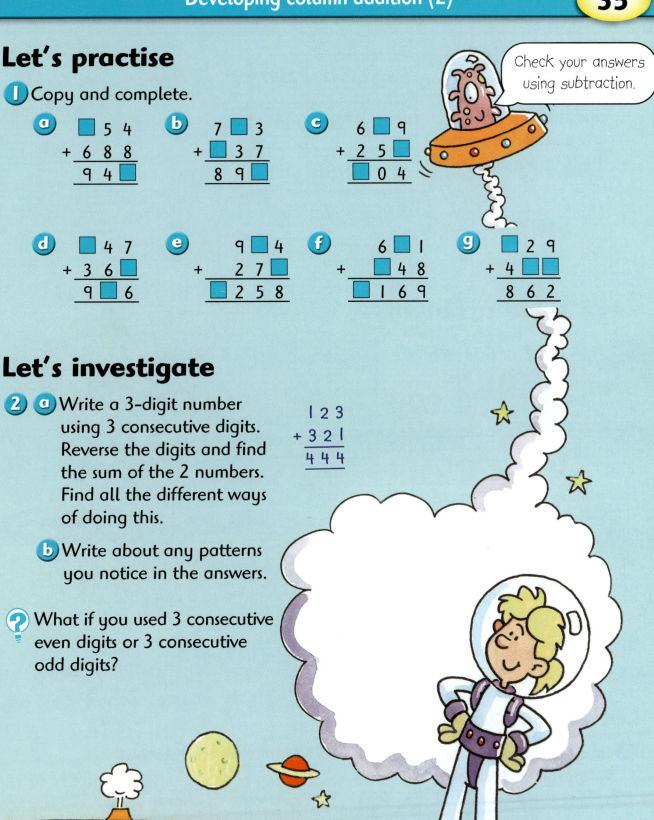

Let's practise

1 Copy the grid.
Find the sum of each row and column, and the total for the grid.

6	542	2347
814	28	9
59	1791	348

Total

Let's solve problems

2
OFFICE EQUIPMENT AND FURNITURE	
printer	£386
computer	£1378
chair	£187
desk	£218
filing cabinet	£67

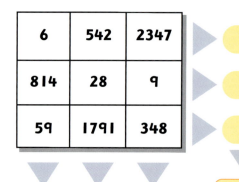

Find how much these people spent.

a Mr Singh bought a computer, a desk and a chair.

b Mrs Thomas bought 2 chairs, a filing cabinet and a computer.

c Ms Gair bought a printer, 2 filing cabinets and a chair.

d Mr Dillon spent £791. Which 3 things did he buy?

Let's investigate

3 Investigate adding 3 of these numbers to make different totals.
Record your additions.

 564   787   385   439

? What if you added only 2 of the numbers?
How many different totals are there now?

Let's practise

Find the totals.

1. (a) £9·62 and £14·36　　(b) £3·86 and £13·58
   (c) £4·37 and £9·22　　(d) £8·78 and £12·07
   (e) £10·47 and £6·93　　(f) £20·08 and £13·38

Let's investigate

2. (a) Investigate using 4 of these digits to make 2 decimal numbers.

| 2 | 6 | 7 | 8 | 4 |　　2·7 + 8·4 = 11·1

Add each pair of numbers and record the answer.
Find as many different totals as you can.

   (b) Explain why some totals are the same.

3. Mrs Kahn buys 3 of these items.

| can of tomatoes 0·44 kg | sugar 1·10 kg | jam 0·28 kg | potatoes 4·55 kg | washing powder 3·80 kg |

Investigate the different total masses in her shopping basket.
Record each addition.

? What if Mrs Kahn bought 4 of the items?

Let's practise

1 Use any method of column subtraction to find the answers.

a 754 − 287 = ☐   **b** 831 − 758 = ☐   **c** 904 − 368 = ☐

d 819 − 436 = ☐   **e** 923 − 654 = ☐   **f** 803 − 581 = ☐

g 711 − 284 = ☐   **h** 419 − 826 = ☐   **i** 555 − 103 = ☐

Check your answers using addition.

Let's play   A game for 2

You need

3 dice each

Decide who is Player 1 and who is Player 2.

- Each player rolls their dice and creates a 3-digit number.

3   6   6   2   1   3

- Each player finds the difference between the 2 numbers.
- Player 1's score is the number of 3s in the answer.
- Player 2's score is the number of 4s in the answer.

```
    366
  − 213
    153
```

Player 1 scores 1
Player 2 scores 0

The winner is the first player to score 10 points.

? What if the 2 numbers were added?
Player 1 scores a point for each 7 in the answer, and
Player 2 scores a point for each 8 in the answer.

Let's practise

1 Copy and complete.

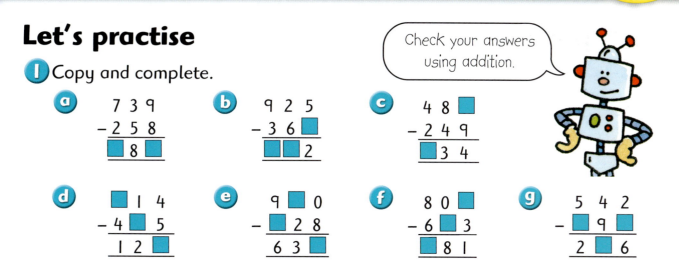

Check your answers using addition.

a
```
    7 3 9
  - 2 5 8
  ☐ 8 ☐
```

b
```
    9 2 5
  - 3 6 ☐
  ☐ ☐ 2
```

c
```
    4 8 ☐
  - 2 4 9
  ☐ 3 4
```

d
```
  ☐ 1 4
  - 4 ☐ 5
    1 2 ☐
```

e
```
    9 ☐ 0
  - ☐ 2 8
    6 3 ☐
```

f
```
    8 0 ☐
  - 6 ☐ 3
  ☐ 8 1
```

g
```
    5 4 2
  - ☐ 9 ☐
    2 ☐ 6
```

Let's investigate

2 Choose 3 different digits from the cards to make a 3-digit number.

1	2	3
4	5	6
7	8	9

- Reverse the digits to make a different 3-digit number.
- Find the difference between the 2 numbers.

```
    834
  - 438
    396
```

- Do this 10 times.
- Write the differences in order, smallest first.
- Write about any patterns in the differences.

? What if 2 of the 3 digits were the same?

Let's practise

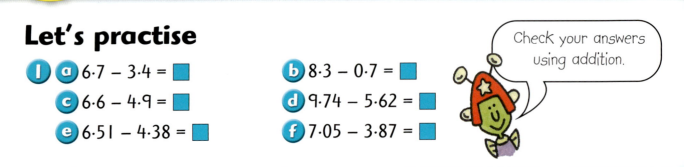

1. (a) 6·7 − 3·4 = ☐
   (b) 8·3 − 0·7 = ☐
   (c) 6·6 − 4·9 = ☐
   (d) 9·74 − 5·62 = ☐
   (e) 6·51 − 4·38 = ☐
   (f) 7·05 − 3·87 = ☐

Check your answers using addition.

Let's solve problems

2. These are the prices of the same items in 2 shops.

Space-Is-Us

Alien gel	£4·37
Star stickers	£6·27
Toy robot	£7·89
Planets book	£9·25
Space rocket	£12·42
Telescope	£13·42

Space Place

Alien gel	£3·79
Star stickers	£5·36
Toy robot	£8·12
Planets book	£8·88
Space rocket	£11·74
Telescope	£11·86

(a) For each item, find the difference between the prices in the 2 shops.

(b) Which item has the largest difference?

(c) If you bought the Alien gel and the Toy robot from both shops, which shop would be cheaper, and by how much?

3. Jed is training to run the 100 metres. The times show how he has improved over 5 months.

By how much do Jed's times improve each month?

May	17·64 seconds
June	16·89 seconds
July	15·02 seconds
August	14·47 seconds
September	14·06 seconds

Let's practise 🖩

1 **a** £6·30 + 85p = ☐

b £7·25 + 30p = ☐

c £7·06 + £1·34 = ☐

d £4·09 + £7·41 = ☐

e 78p + £42·80 = ☐

f £27·78 + £10·02 = ☐

2 Use your calculator as a function machine.
These are your input numbers.

a 12   **b** 13   **c** 14   **d** 5   **e** 16   **f** 17

Enter a number and press ÷ 3 x 3 = .
Your output is displayed on the calculator screen.

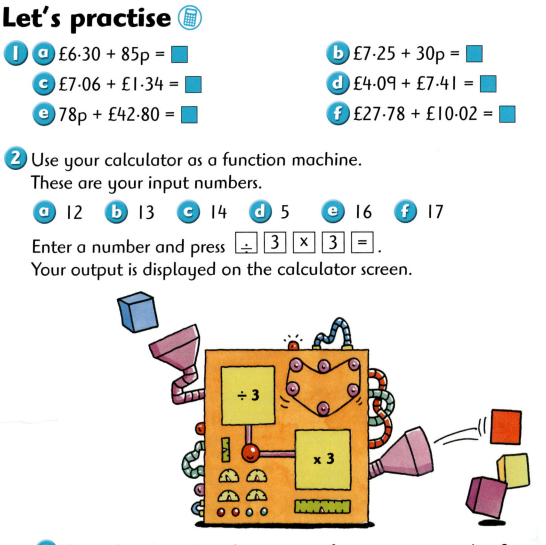

g What do you notice about some of your output numbers?

h Why does this happen?

Let's investigate 🖩

3 Here is a function machine.

- Use your calculator to investigate the results for different input numbers.

- Record each input and output.

- Write about any patterns you notice.

Let's practise

1. Copy the calculations.

   a 3685 − 978 = 2677   **b** 4871 − 379 = 4492   **c** 7982 − 268 = 7614

   d 8456 − 554 = 7802   **e** 5895 − 458 = 5437   **f** 9454 − 647 = 8807

   Pretend that the ☐ − key on your calculator is broken.
   Check the answers on your calculator, without using the ☐ − key.
   Tick the correct answers.

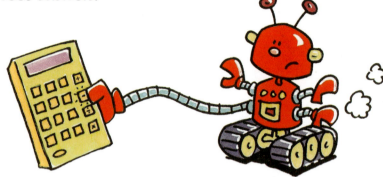

2. Write 'odd' or 'even' for the answers to the questions **without** working
   them out.

   a 142 + 517   **b** 642 + 816   **c** 737 + 403

   d 812 + 389   **e** 763 − 172   **f** 495 − 131

   g 486 − 294   **h** 674 − 431   **i** 985 − 240

   Choose any 5 questions from **a** to **i** and explain why you know the
   answer will be odd or even.

Let's investigate

385   198   346   281

3. Investigate odd or even answers.

   - Choose 2 numbers from above to make an addition and a subtraction.
   - Predict each answer as an odd or an even number.
   - Calculate the answers.
   - Were your predictions correct?
   - Do this as many times as you can.

   ❓ What if you chose 3 numbers from the box to make an addition?

Let's practise

1. Copy the calculations.
   Write +, −, x or ÷ to make each calculation correct.

   a) 319 ☐ 275 = 594   b) 24 ☐ 68 = 1632

   c) 651 ☐ 217 = 3   d) 514 ☐ 48 = 466

   e) (18 ☐ 3) ☐ 6 = 60   f) 90 ☐ (40 ☐ 8) = 85

Let's solve problems

2. Rocky Driver delivers supernova
   sweets to different space stations.

   Radek — 583 km — Warck
   Radek — 374 km — Galina
   Galina — 251 km — Warck
   Radek — 442 km — Taiko
   Galina — 276 km — Taiko
   Galina — 598 km — Hara
   Warck — 537 km — Hara
   Taiko — 1058 km — Hara

   a) How many
      kilometres did
      Rocky travel
      each day?

Travel log	
Monday	From Radek, to Galina, to Warck.
Tuesday	Left Warck for Taiko, then back to Galina.
Wednesday	From Galina to Warck, then to Hara.
Thursday	From Hara to Taiko and then back to Radek.

   b) To which space stations did
      Rocky travel?

   I set off from Taiko and travelled to two
   other planets. I travelled 650 km in total.

   c) Rocky travelled directly from Warck to Hara.
      How many kilometres less is this than if he went via Taiko?

   d) Rocky travelled from Taiko directly to Radek.
      How many kilometres less is this than if he went via Galina?

Let's solve problems

1 Two teachers were photocopying sheets for their lessons.

a One week, Mrs Bendall copied 35 science sheets, 78 English sheets and 64 maths sheets. How many photocopied sheets were there?

b If Mrs Bendall copied the same number once a week for 3 weeks, how many photocopied sheets is that?

c One week, Mr Paulo copied 27 science sheets, 48 English sheets and 63 maths sheets. How many photocopied sheets were there?

d If Mr Paulo copied the same number once a week for 3 weeks, how many photocopied sheets is that?

e How many fewer photocopied sheets does Mr Paulo have than Mrs Bendall during 3 weeks?

f What is the total number of photocopied sheets made by both teachers over 3 weeks?

2 There are 2 types of alien on the planet Zog: Zoglans and Zogglets. Zoglans have 2 heads and 2 legs, Zogglets have 1 head and 3 legs. There are 59 aliens in total. How many of each type of alien are there if there are:

a 83 heads　　**b** 161 legs?

Let's investigate

3 Investigate 3-digit totals of two 2-digit consecutive numbers.

57 + 58 = 115

a Record your additions.

b What do you notice about all the answers?

c Explain why.

? What if you found totals of three 2-digit consecutive numbers?

Let's practise

①

| 48p | £3·75 | £9·38 | 88p |

Choose 2 cards and find the total.
Repeat for 5 other pairs of cards.

Let's solve problems

②

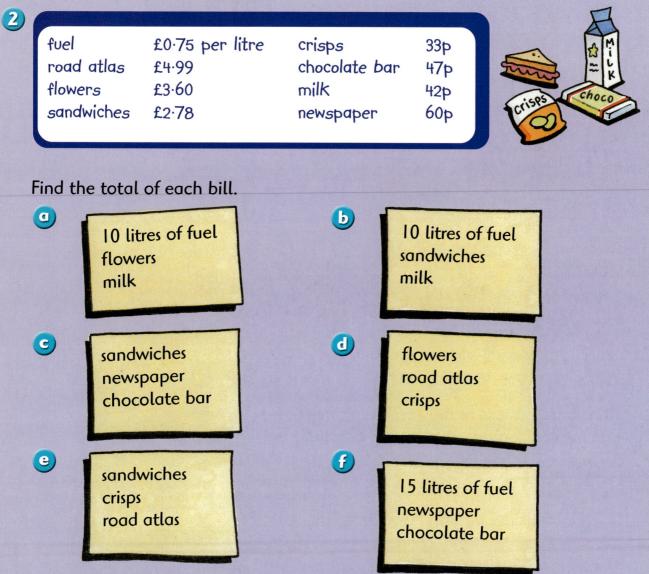

fuel	£0·75 per litre	crisps	33p
road atlas	£4·99	chocolate bar	47p
flowers	£3·60	milk	42p
sandwiches	£2·78	newspaper	60p

Find the total of each bill.

a
10 litres of fuel
flowers
milk

b
10 litres of fuel
sandwiches
milk

c
sandwiches
newspaper
chocolate bar

d
flowers
road atlas
crisps

e
sandwiches
crisps
road atlas

f
15 litres of fuel
newspaper
chocolate bar

g Mrs Hill spent £9·06 on 3 items. What were they?

h Mr Murray spent £15·87 on 4 items. One of the items was a newspaper.
What were the other items?

Let's practise

1
a 50% of £230 = ☐   **b** 25% of £160 = ☐   **c** 10% of £240 = ☐

d 50% of 150 = ☐   **e** 25% of 300 = ☐   **f** 10% of 34 = ☐

Let's play   A game for 2

| 50% | 25% | 20% | 10% |

You need

4 cards labelled with the percentages shown

- Copy the grid.
- Take turns to choose a percentage card and a number from the grid.
- Find the percentage of the number and record it.
  25% of 40 = 10
- If the answer is on the grid, score 1 point.
- The winner is the first player to score 8 points.

400	9	50	60
12	20	360	90
10	5	120	40
36	180	18	6

Let's solve problems

2 760 aliens are travelling to the planet Zog. Some are Zoglans, the rest are Zogglets.

a If 20% are Zoglans, how many are:
- Zoglans
- Zogglets?

b If 30% are Zoglans, how many are:
- Zoglans
- Zogglets?

c If 40% are Zogglets, how many are:
- Zoglans
- Zogglets?

d If 90% are Zogglets, how many are:
- Zoglans
- Zogglets?

Let's practise

1 Copy and complete each question in 2 ways.
Draw loops to show which numbers you multiplied first.

Example:

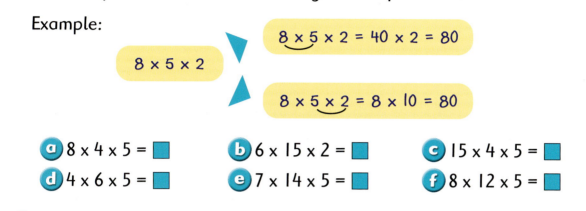

8 × 5 × 2

8 × 5 × 2 = 40 × 2 = 80

8 × 5 × 2 = 8 × 10 = 80

a 8 × 4 × 5 = ☐

d 4 × 6 × 5 = ☐

b 6 × 15 × 2 = ☐

e 7 × 14 × 5 = ☐

c 15 × 4 × 5 = ☐

f 8 × 12 × 5 = ☐

2 Copy and complete by placing an even number in the calculation and then finding the answer.
Repeat 5 times, each time with a different even number.

a 15 × ☐ × 5 = ☐

b 12 × ☐ × 2·5 = ☐

3 Write as many multiplications as you can with these answers.

a 36

b 72

c 96

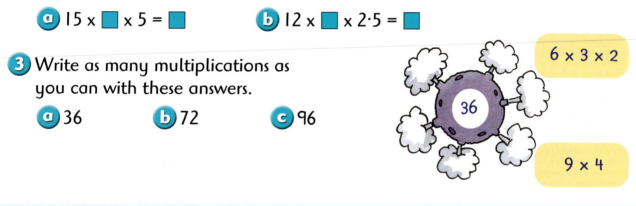

6 × 3 × 2

36

9 × 4

Let's investigate

4 **a** Which 3 of these numbers have a product of 495?

b Investigate different products of 3 of the numbers.
 ● What is the smallest odd product?
 ● What is the greatest even product?

c Find the smallest and largest product of 4 of the numbers.

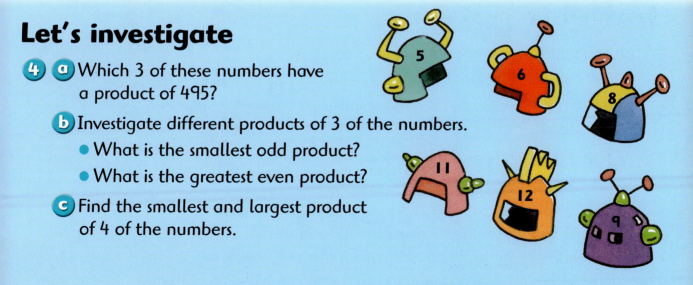

Let's practise

1. (a) $14 \times 5 = \square$ (b) $16 \times 4 = \square$ (c) $13 \times 6 = \square$
   (d) $22 \times 6 = \square$ (e) $31 \times 4 = \square$ (f) $27 \times 3 = \square$

Let's solve problems

2. Jack planted 4 rows of seeds with 5 seeds in each row.
   He used 20 seeds.
   He wrote what he had done in 6 number statements.

   | $4 \times 5 = 20$ | $5 \times 4 = 20$ | $20 \div 5 = 4$ | $20 \div 4 = 5$ |

   | $4 + 4 + 4 + 4 + 4 = 20$ | $5 + 5 + 5 + 5 = 20$ |

   Write 6 number statements for each of these stories.

   (a) 27 chairs were arranged in rows.
   There were 3 rows with 9 chairs
   in each row.

   (b) In the car park, 32 space buggies
   were in 4 rows with 8 space
   buggies in each row.

3. (a) Bryn used 3 of the
   numbers from the
   rocket trail to make
   2 multiplications and
   2 divisions.

   > 63   7   3
   > 441
   > 21   189   147

   | $3 \times 7 = 2$ | $17 \times 3 = 21$ |
   | $21 \div 3 = 7$ | $21 \div 7 = 3$ |

   Find 3 numbers in the rocket trail to make
   2 different multiplications and 2 different divisions.

   (b) Do this 4 more times.

Let's practise

1 **a** 4 × (3 × 5) = ☐   **b** (4 × 3) × 5 = ☐

  c (7 + 4) × 6 = ☐   **d** 7 + (4 × 6) = ☐

  e 8 × (5 − 3) = ☐   **f** (8 × 5) − 3 = ☐

  g (7 × 6) − 2 = ☐   **h** 7 × (6 − 2) = ☐

Solve the part in brackets first.

2 **a** Copy the table.

machine 1		machine 2	
input	output	input	output
5	23	5	
6		6	
7		7	
8		8	

Input the numbers into both machines.

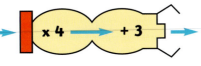

machine 1

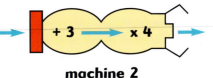

machine 2

Complete the table to show your results.

b Write about why the inputs are the same and the outputs are different.

Let's investigate

3 Investigate making different questions using all these cards.

Examples: 8 × (2 + 4) =   2 + (8 × 4) =

☐ (☐) ☐ 8 ☐ 4

☐ 2 ☐ + ☐ × ☐ =

Which of these answers would you find?

⭐ 24   ⭐ 34   ⭐ 16   ⭐ 20   ⭐ 40   ⭐ 48   ⭐ 8   ⭐ 30

What if ☐ + was replaced by ☐ − ?
Which of the answers can you find now?

Let's practise

1. **a** Share 48 between 4
   b Divide 56 by 8
   c Divide 6 into 66
   d What is 72 divided by 9?
   e How many 3s are in 72?
   f What is 95 divided by 5?

Remember your division and multiplication facts.

2. Which of these number statements are true?
   Copy each true statement.

   a $3 \div 18 = 6$
   $6 \div 18 = 3$
   $18 \div 3 = 6$
   $6 \div 3 = 18$

   b $4 \div 28 = 7$
   $28 \div 4 = 7$
   $28 \div 7 = 4$
   $4 \div 7 = 28$

   c $9 \div 8 = 72$
   $8 \div 9 = 72$
   $72 \div 8 = 9$
   $8 \div 72 = 9$

Let's investigate

3. Make as many correct number statements
   as you can using only these cards.

   $40 \div 4 = 10$

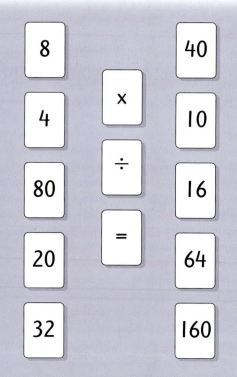

8		40
4	×	10
80	÷	16
20	=	64
32		160

What if all the numbers were 10 times bigger?

Let's practise

1.
a) $\frac{1}{2} = \blacksquare . \blacksquare$

b) $\frac{\blacksquare}{4} = 0.25$

c) $\frac{\blacksquare}{\blacksquare} = 0.1$

d) $\frac{\blacksquare}{\blacksquare} = 0.75$

e) $\frac{3}{10} = 0.\blacksquare$

f) $\frac{\blacksquare}{\blacksquare} = 0.7$

Let's solve problems

2.
a) Four children saved £45·40 between them to go on a trip. They each saved the same amount.
How much did each child save?

b) Five children saved £11·60 between them to go skateboarding. They each saved the same amount.
How much did each child save?

c) Ten children spent a total of £30·50 on holiday. They each spent the same amount. How much did each child spend?

Let's play A game for 2

Take turns to choose a number from the grid.

- Divide it by 4 and write the quotient as a decimal number.

- Your score is the decimal fraction part of your answer.

> 37 ÷ 4 = 9·25 ➜ Score 0·25

- Cover your number with a counter.

The winner is the player with the higher total score when all the numbers are covered.

You need

counters

61	43	31
37	51	52
49	38	47

? What if you divided by 5 instead of 4?

Let's practise

1 Find the answers.

a 9 multiplied by 4

b Triple eight

c Six squared

d The product of 3 and 8

e 12 times 2

f Four lots of 6

g Double 18

h 2 x 9 x 2

i 12 lots of 3

j 3 x 2 x 2 x 2

k Eight threes

l 4 groups of 9

2 Copy the Venn diagram. Sort the numbers from 40 to 80 on the diagram.

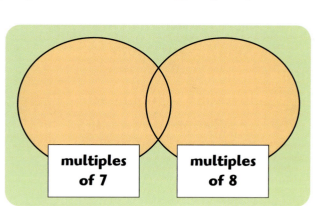

multiples of 7

multiples of 8

3 How many legs have:

a 5 spiders

b 7 flies

c 9 sheep

d 8 three-legged stools?

Let's play   A game for 2

Shuffle the cards and place them face down in a pile.

- Take turns to turn over the top 2 cards and multiply the numbers together.
- That's your score.
- Keep a running total. Use a calculator to help.

The winner is the player with the higher score after all the cards have been turned over.

You need

a pack of playing cards with the picture cards removed

Let's practise

1
(a) ½ of 78
(b) Twice 49
(c) Half of 96

(d) Double 670
(e) Divide 760 by 2
(f) 2 × 860

(g) ½ of 9400
(h) Twice 6500
(i) Halve 14 600

Let's solve problems

2 (a)
Jon is twice as old as Luke.
Jon is 38.
How old is Luke?

(b)
Ali is half as old as Ben.
Ben is 94.
How old is Ali?

(c)
Twice as many people went to watch Rangers as to see Rovers. 8700 went to see Rovers.
How many saw Rangers?

(d)
Laura wants to buy a car.
She has saved £7900.
The car costs double this.
What is the price of the car?

(e)
Dave has twice as many stamps as Dan. Dave has 72.
How many has Dan?

(f)
Josie is half as old as Dan. Josie is 42.
How old is Dan?

Let's investigate

3 The sum of 3 different multiples of 10 is double the sum of 2 different multiples of 10.
Both sums are greater than 100 and less than 400.
Investigate which different sums can be made.

> 90 + 150 + 60 = 300
> 80 + 70 = 150
> 300 is double 150

? What if the numbers were multiples of 100 and the sums were between 1000 and 4000?

Let's practise

Use doubling to help you.

1 Copy and complete these patterns.

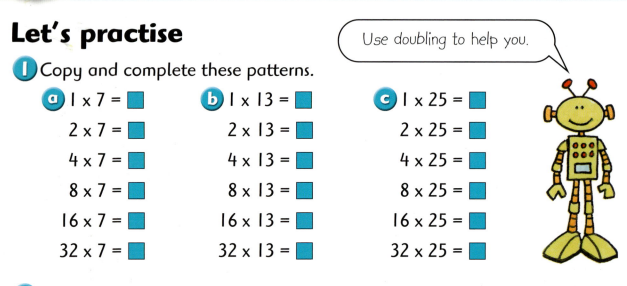

a) 1 x 7 = ☐
2 x 7 = ☐
4 x 7 = ☐
8 x 7 = ☐
16 x 7 = ☐
32 x 7 = ☐

b) 1 x 13 = ☐
2 x 13 = ☐
4 x 13 = ☐
8 x 13 = ☐
16 x 13 = ☐
32 x 13 = ☐

c) 1 x 25 = ☐
2 x 25 = ☐
4 x 25 = ☐
8 x 25 = ☐
16 x 25 = ☐
32 x 25 = ☐

2 Start with this fact: **1 x 75 = 75**.

- Double the first number to create a new question.
- Find the answer.
- Keep doubling the first number of each new question.
- Find each answer.
- What is 64 x 75?

3 The diagram shows that the multiplications 16 x 5 and 8 x 10 are a matching pair.

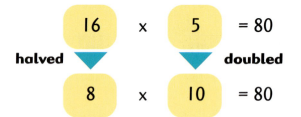

halved   16   x   5   = 80   doubled

8   x   10   = 80

Find the matching pairs in this set of multiplications.
Draw a diagram for each pair.

a) 100 x 9   **b)** 6 x 90   **c)** 12 x 45   **d)** 7 x 70
e) 14 x 25   **f)** 50 x 18   **g)** 35 x 8   **h)** 14 x 35
i) 70 x 4   **j)** 15 x 16   **k)** 7 x 50   **l)** 30 x 8

Let's investigate

4 Write out the 3 times table.
Investigate how doubling can produce first multiples of 6, then multiples of 12.

Let's practise

1 This machine finds factors of numbers.
Find all the factors of each number.

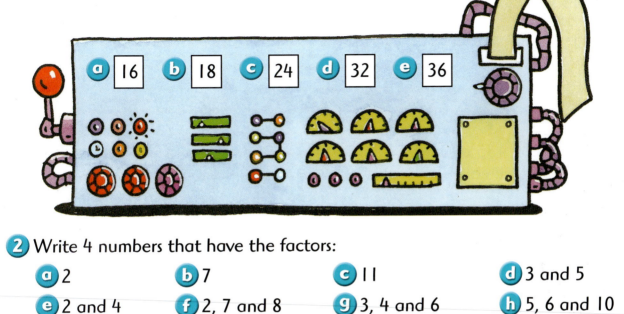

a 16 **b** 18 **c** 24 **d** 32 **e** 36

2 Write 4 numbers that have the factors:

a 2   **b** 7   **c** 11   **d** 3 and 5

e 2 and 4   **f** 2, 7 and 8   **g** 3, 4 and 6   **h** 5, 6 and 10

Let's investigate

3 This calculator has broken keys.
The only ones working are the ones shown.
Angus made 35 by pressing 4 keys:

5 × 7 = 35

Tap

Investigate making numbers using × , = and 2 of the working digit keys.
Record your findings.

? What if you used × , = and 3 or 4 of the working digit keys?

Let's practise

1. **a** 15 × 10 = ☐　　**b** 27 × 10 = ☐　　**c** 44 × 10 = ☐

   d 15 × 9 = ☐　　**e** 27 × 9 = ☐　　**f** 44 × 9 = ☐

   g 15 × 11 = ☐　　**h** 27 × 11 = ☐　　**i** 44 × 11 = ☐

Let's solve problems

2 Chewies cost 13p each. Jim buys 40
chewies, which cost him a total of £5·20.

   a How much do 41 chewies cost?

   b How much do 39 chewies cost?

3 Clare buys 20 sweets at 9p each,
costing a total of £1·80.

   a How much do 41 sweets cost?

   b How much do 39 sweets cost?

Let's investigate

*Make use of facts that are
closely related.*

4 Copy the 3 incomplete multiplications.

   19 × ☐ =

   20 × ☐ =

   21 × ☐ =

- Use the same 2-digit number in each box to complete them.
- Find the answers.
- Do this 5 times using a different 2-digit number each time.
- Write about how you found the answers.

❓ What if the 3 numbers were 29, 30 and 31 instead of 19, 20 and 21?

Let's practise

1 Here is a way of finding the answer to 15 × 6.

$$15 \times 6 = (10 \times 6) + (5 \times 6)$$
$$= \quad 60 \quad + \quad 30$$
$$= \quad 90$$

Copy and complete.

a 27 × 5 = ☐   **b** 31 × 4 = ☐   **c** 26 × 5 = ☐

d 26 × 7 = ☐   **e** 39 × 5 = ☐   **f** 38 × 6 = ☐

g 42 × 7 = ☐   **h** 46 × 8 = ☐   **i** 48 × 9 = ☐

Let's solve problems

2 Carlos has gone shopping. Work out how much he will pay for each item on his list.

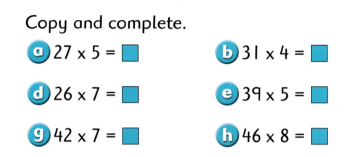

37p   32p   43p   48p   56p

a 4 packs of butter

b 8 tins of beans

c 6 yoghurts

d 7 bars of chocolate

e 5 loaves of bread

Let's play **A game for 2**

- Player 1 is 'less than 200'.
  Player 2 is 'more than 200'.

- Each player chooses an asteroid number.
  Each player rolls the dice and multiplies their asteroid number by their dice throw.

- For each answer less than 200, player 1 scores a point.
  For each answer more than 200, player 2 scores a point.

The winner is the first to reach 5 points.

You need

a 1–10 dice

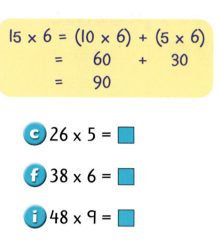

26   29   41   35   38   44

Let's practise

1 **a** $72 \div 6 = \square$ **b** $6 \times \square = 72$ **c** $\frac{1}{6}$ of $72 = \square$

d $12 \times \square = 72$ **e** $\square \div 12 = 6$ **f** $\frac{\square}{\square}$ of $72 = 6$

2 **a** Choose a number from the space rocket and a fraction from the asteroid. Find the answer.

$$\frac{1}{2} \text{ of } 120 = 60$$

b Write 5 related facts using the 3 numbers.

$\frac{1}{2}$ of $120 = 60$ $2 \times 60 = 120$
$120 \div 2 = 60$ $120 \div 60 = 2$
$60 \times 2 = 120$

Do this 10 times.

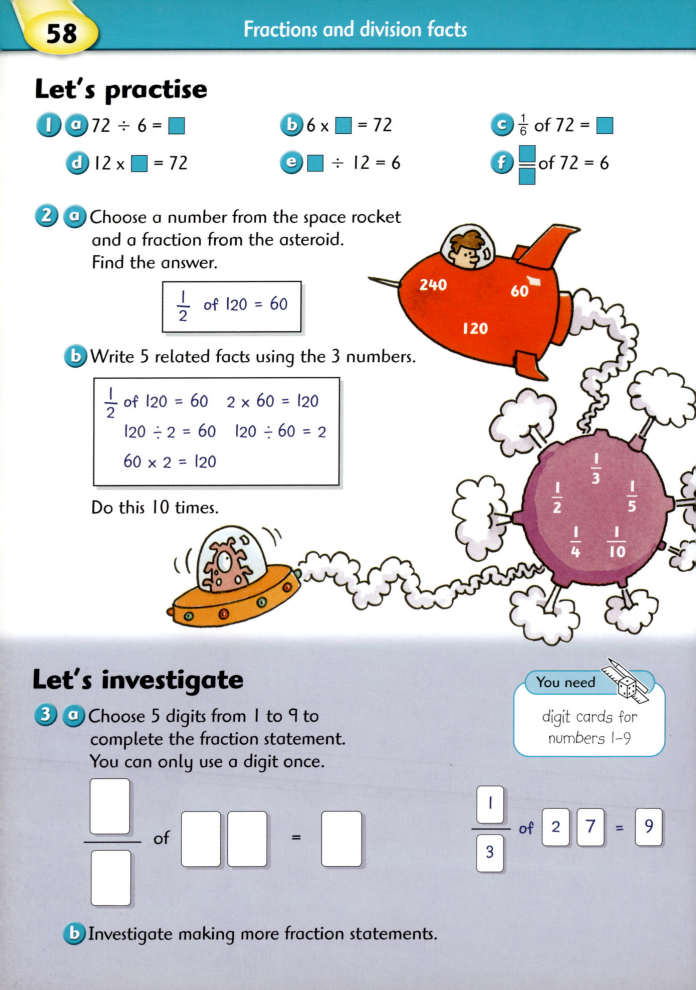

240 60 120

$\frac{1}{3}$ $\frac{1}{2}$ $\frac{1}{5}$ $\frac{1}{4}$ $\frac{1}{10}$

Let's investigate

3 **a** Choose 5 digits from 1 to 9 to complete the fraction statement. You can only use a digit once.

$\frac{\square}{\square}$ of $\square\square = \square$

$\frac{1}{3}$ of $2\ 7 = 9$

You need
digit cards for numbers 1–9

b Investigate making more fraction statements.

Let's practise

1
a 60 x 6 = ☐
b 4 x 70 = ☐
c 80 x 7 = ☐
d 7 x 60 = ☐
e 30 x 70 = ☐
f 40 x 50 = ☐
g 70 x 90 = ☐
h 80 x 90 = ☐

2 Jade finds the answer to 27 x 4 like this:

	20	7	
4	80	28	= 108

Copy and complete.

a 46 x 5 = ☐
b 23 x 6 = ☐
c 38 x 4 = ☐
d 47 x 7 = ☐
e 52 x 8 = ☐
f 54 x 9 = ☐

3 Jonas finds the answer to 254 x 5 like this:

	200	50	4	
5	1000	250	20	= 1270

Copy and complete.

a 237 x 4 = ☐
b 265 x 5 = ☐
c 324 x 6 = ☐
d 352 x 7 = ☐
e 402 x 8 = ☐
f 538 x 9 = ☐

Let's play   A game for 2

You need

a set of 0 to 9 digit cards

- Place the cards face down in a pile.
- Each player turns over 4 cards and makes a 3-digit by 1-digit multiplication.
- Both players work out their answer.
- The player whose total is nearer 3000 scores a point.

The winner is the first player to score 5 points.

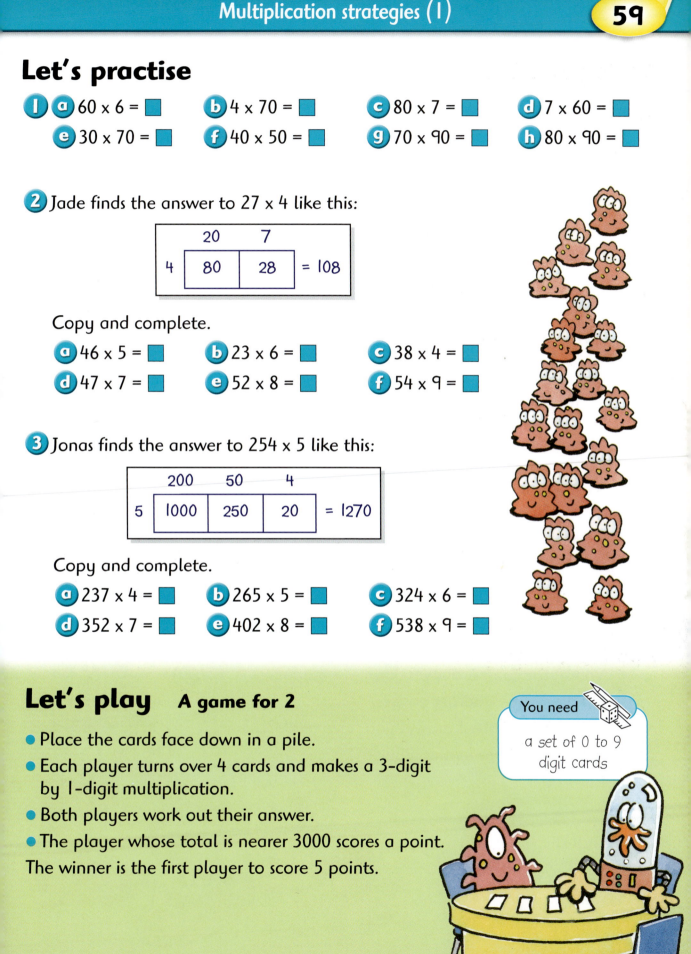

Let's practise

1 Megan is multiplying on paper.
Look at her method.

```
    5 1 4
  ×     3
  1 5 4 2
        1
```

```
    3 7 1
  ×     4
  1 4 8 4
      2
```

```
    3 4 6
  ×     9
  3 1 1 4
      4 5
```

Copy and complete.

a
```
    1 1 3
  ×     5
```

b
```
    3 1 7
  ×     4
```

c
```
    3 1 6
  ×     9
```

d
```
    2 5 3
  ×     3
```

e
```
    5 6 2
  ×     4
```

f
```
    5 4 1
  ×     8
```

2 What is the difference between 444 × 4 and 555 × 5?

Let's investigate

3 Choose 4 digits from the spaceships to make
a 3-digit and a 1-digit number.
Find their product.

659 × 3

- Investigate making more products.
- What is the largest answer you have made?
- Can you make a larger answer?
- What is the smallest answer you have made?
- Can you make a smaller answer?

? What if the set of
digits was 0 to 9,
not 1 to 9?

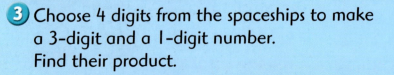

Let's practise

1 Kalil is multiplying on paper. Look at his method.

```
      2·5          9·1          9·4
  ×     3      ×     4      ×     7
      7·5        3 6·4       6 5·8
      1                        2
```

Copy and complete.

a
```
      8·3
  ×     4
```

b
```
      7·4
  ×     4
```

c
```
      5·5
  ×     6
```

d
```
      7·3
  ×     5
```

e
```
      8·1
  ×     4
```

f
```
      6·7
  ×     8
```

g
```
      9·3
  ×     7
```

h
```
      9·7
  ×     5
```

2 What is the difference between:

a 1·1 × 1 and 2·2 × 2

b 2·2 × 2 and 3·3 × 3

c 3·3 × 3 and 4·4 × 4

d 4·4 × 4 and 5·5 × 5?

Let's investigate

3 Choose 3 digits from the space helmets to make a 2-digit decimal number and a 1-digit number. Find their product.

Example: 2·6 × 3

- Investigate making more products.
- Which of your products is nearest to 50?
- If possible, make a product nearer to 50.
- Which of your products is furthest from 50?
- If possible, make a product further from 50.

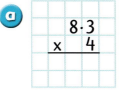
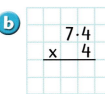
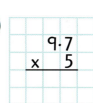
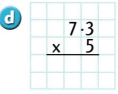
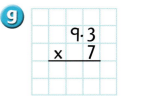
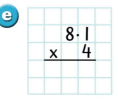
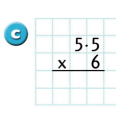

What if the set of digits included 0?

Let's practise

1 **a** 6 x 2 = ☐
6 x 20 = ☐
60 x 2 = ☐
60 x 20 = ☐

b 5 x 8 = ☐
5 x 80 = ☐
50 x 8 = ☐
50 x 80 = ☐

c 4 x 9 = ☐
4 x 90 = ☐
40 x 9 = ☐
40 x 90 = ☐

2 Oliver found the answer to 36 x 54 like this:

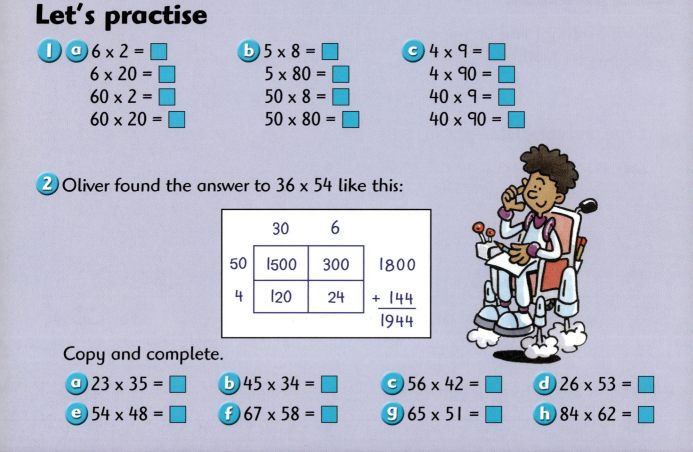

	30	6	
50	1500	300	1800
4	120	24	+ 144
			1944

Copy and complete.

a 23 x 35 = ☐   **b** 45 x 34 = ☐   **c** 56 x 42 = ☐   **d** 26 x 53 = ☐

e 54 x 48 = ☐   **f** 67 x 58 = ☐   **g** 65 x 51 = ☐   **h** 84 x 62 = ☐

Let's investigate

3 Investigate using the 4 digits in the asteroids to make two 2-digit numbers.
Find the products.

- What is the largest answer you have found?
- Find, if possible, an answer that is larger.

? What if the 4 digits made a 3-digit by 1-digit multiplication?

32 x 45

Let's practise

1 This is how Anita divided 176 by 5.

```
        3 5 r 1
  5)  1 7 6
    - 1 5 0      (3 0 × 5)
        2 6
      - 2 5      (5 × 5)
          1
```

Check your answers using multiplication and a calculator.

Copy and complete, using the same written method.

a 168 ÷ 3 = ☐   **b** 262 ÷ 3 = ☐   **c** 296 ÷ 4 = ☐   **d** 371 ÷ 6 = ☐

e 553 ÷ 5 = ☐   **f** 486 ÷ 6 = ☐   **g** 359 ÷ 4 = ☐   **h** 568 ÷ 6 = ☐

Let's solve problems

2 Use your answers from question 1 to help you solve these problems.

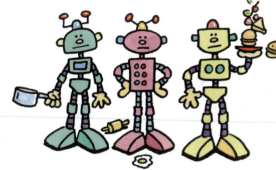

a Dad spent £1·68 on 3 jars of jam. How much was 1 jar?

b Mum has £2·96 in change. If she shares it between her 4 children, how much do they each get?

c Dave saved the same amount of money each week for 6 weeks. Altogether he saved £48·60. How much did he save each week?

Let's investigate

3 Choose 3 of the digits to make a 3-digit number.
- Divide your number by 6.
- What is the remainder?
- Investigate making different 3-digit numbers and dividing them by 6.
- Sort your 3-digit numbers according to the remainders when they are divided by 6.
- Why are the remainders always even?

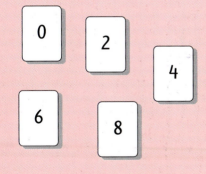

0   2   4   6   8

? What if the digits were   1   3   5   7   9   ?

Let's practise

1. a) 20 x 30 = ☐   b) 25 x 20 = ☐   c) 20 x 40 = ☐   d) 25 x 30 = ☐

   e) 40 x 25 = ☐   f) 30 x 30 = ☐   g) 50 x 20 = ☐   h) 25 x 50 = ☐

2. Khalid found an approximate answer to 19 x 32 like this:

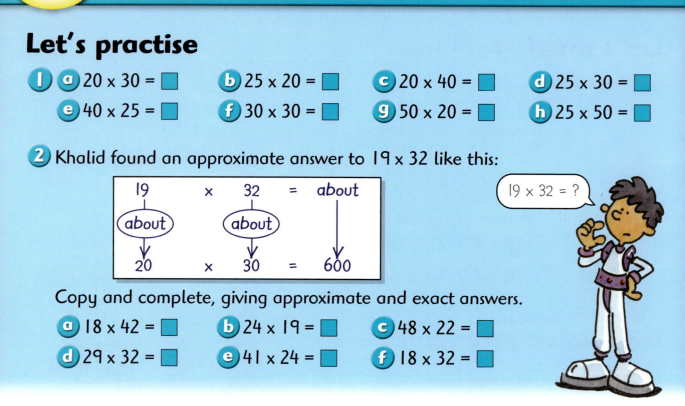

19 x 32 = ?

Copy and complete, giving approximate and exact answers.

   a) 18 x 42 = ☐   b) 24 x 19 = ☐   c) 48 x 22 = ☐

   d) 29 x 32 = ☐   e) 41 x 24 = ☐   f) 18 x 32 = ☐

Let's solve problems

3. Ahmed delivers bread all over the country.
   Copy and complete the table.

City	Distance (miles)	Number of journeys	Approximate mileage	Actual mileage
Leeds	46	19		
Bristol	57	21		
York	63	19		
Cardiff	68	21		

Let's investigate

4. Tyler made these two 2-digit numbers with the digit cards.
   He found their product.

   8 1

   2 9

   28 x 19 = 532

   - Investigate other products of two 2-digit numbers using each
     digit card once each time.
   - Find the pairs of numbers with the smallest and largest product.

   ❓ What if products of a 3-digit and a 1-digit number were
   found using the same digit cards?

Let's solve problems

1 Find 2 numbers with:

   a a product of 160 and a difference of 36

   b a sum of 25 and a product of 114.

2 There are 203 children in 7 classes.
The number of children in every class is usually the same.
How many children are in Class B,
if 4 children from this class are away?

3 Carl will be 13 next year.
His grandad is 6 times older than he is.
How old is his grandad?

4 Molly thinks of a number.
She adds 6 to it and divides this by 9.
Her answer is 6.
What was the number she thought of?

5 Mrs Brown has drawn a plan of the
school hall. It shows the layout of
chairs for a school performance.
How many chairs are needed
altogether?

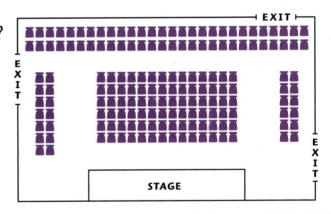

Let's investigate

6 Put the same number in the first box of each calculation.

$$4 \times \boxed{} = \boxed{} \qquad\qquad 400 + \boxed{} = \boxed{}$$

- Investigate the differences between the 2 answers for different missing numbers.
- When is the difference the least?

 What if the 2 calculations were $2 \times \boxed{}$ and $200 + \boxed{}$?

Let's solve problems

1. Pete bought nine 27p stamps. He used 3 of them.
   How many pence worth of stamps has he now?

2. A jacket and a skirt cost £51. If the jacket costs twice as
   much as the skirt, what are the prices of the 2 items?

3.

   Cheaptalk
   26p per minute

   Easy chat
   35p per minute

   QUICK CHAT
   47p per minute

   How much would it cost to talk on each mobile phone for:

   a. 2 minutes
   b. 5 minutes
   c. 26 minutes?

4. Which amounts of money between £1 and £1·50 have a
   remainder of 1p when shared between 5 people?

5. One litre of unleaded petrol costs 72·4p. How much is 5 litres?

6. Use a calculator to find how much is spent in 1 year on medicines,
   laundry and meals in the Wellbeing Hospital.

   a. £24 000 per month
      on medicines

   b. £6000 per week
      on laundry

   c. £800 per day
      on meals

Let's investigate

7. You have three 35p and four 25p stamps.
   Investigate all the different amounts you
   could stick on a parcel.

Let's practise

1 Copy these statements.
Use **+**, **−**, **x**, **÷** or **=** to make them correct.

a 456 ◯ 238 = 218

b 69 ◯ 5 = 345

c 512 ◯ 4 = 128

d 217 ◯ 22 = 195

e 89 ◯ 7 ◯ 20 = 603

f 432 ◯ 9 ◯ 48 ◯ 96

g 27 ◯ 12 ◯ 18 = 18

h 176 ◯ 139 ◯ 15 = 21

Let's solve problems

2 120 women and 40 men were surveyed in a supermarket.
Work out the number of people in each statement.

a 90% of women said they shop at least once a week.

b 30% of women said they prefer brown bread to white.

c 40% of men said they prefer washing powder to tablets.

d 80% of men said they bought chocolate every week.

e 25% of women said they were vegetarian.

f 5% of women said they didn't like cheese.

g 55% of men said they prefer white bread to brown.

h 95% of men said they liked ice cream.

Let's practise

1. If 1 euro is about 0·60 pounds, approximately how many pounds is:

   a 2 euros **b** 3 euros **c** 5 euros

   d 10 euros **e** 17 euros **f** 22 euros?

2.

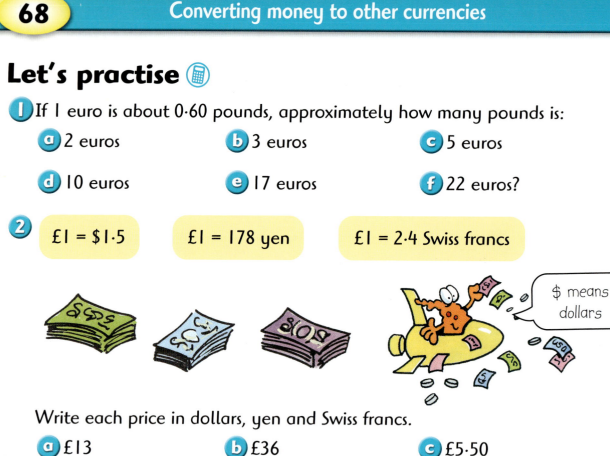

£1 = $1·5   £1 = 178 yen   £1 = 2·4 Swiss francs

$ means dollars

Write each price in dollars, yen and Swiss francs.

   a £13 **b** £36 **c** £5·50

   d £7·30 **e** £6·80 **f** £11·40

Let's solve problems

£1 = 178 yen

£1 = $1·5

3. Ella was going on holiday. She had £130 and wanted to changed it to yen. The bank charged a fee.

   a If she was given 20 915 yen, how much was the fee in yen?

   b How much was the fee in pounds?

4. Jack is going on holiday. He has £100 and wants to change it to dollars. The bank charges a fee.

   a If he was given $135, how much was the fee in dollars?

   b How much was the fee in pounds?

Let's practise

$1.7 \text{ km} = 1 \text{ km } 700 \text{ m} = 1700 \text{ m}$

1 Write in metres.

  a 2·3 km   **b** $5\frac{1}{2}$ km   **c** 10·1 km   **d** 15·8 km

  e 0·7 km   **f** $\frac{9}{10}$ km   **g** $3\frac{1}{4}$ km   **h** $7\frac{3}{4}$ km

2 For each length, draw and complete a mm–cm–m diagram.

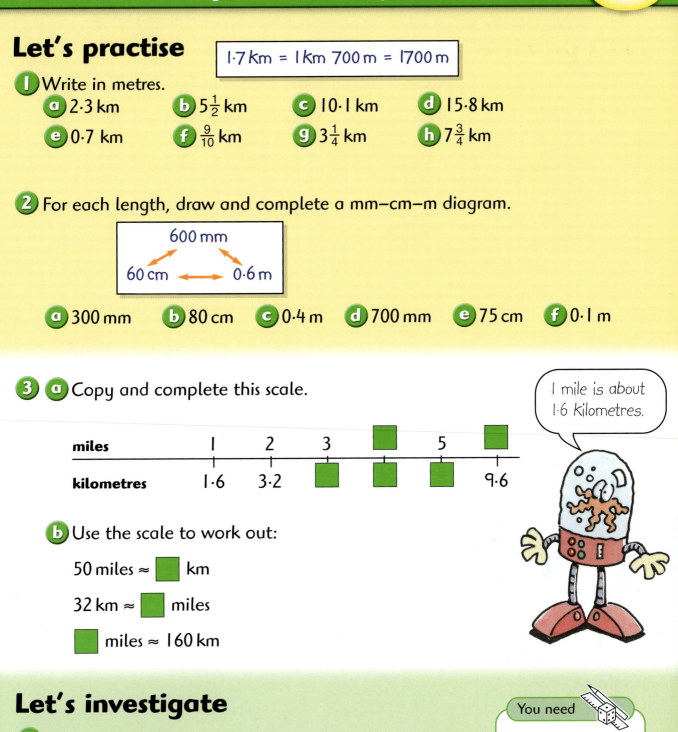

600 mm

60 cm   0·6 m

  a 300 mm   **b** 80 cm   **c** 0·4 m   **d** 700 mm   **e** 75 cm   **f** 0·1 m

3 **a** Copy and complete this scale.

miles	1	2	3	⬜	5	⬜
kilometres	1·6	3·2	⬜	⬜	⬜	9·6

1 mile is about 1·6 kilometres.

  b Use the scale to work out:

50 miles ≈ ⬜ km

32 km ≈ ⬜ miles

⬜ miles ≈ 160 km

Let's investigate

4 Copy the spiral. Continue the spiral as far as you can. Copy and complete the table.

You need

5 mm squared paper, a ruler

Number of lines	Total length of lines
1	5 mm
2	15 mm
3	30 mm

Let's practise

1 Write the measurement shown by each arrow to the nearest millimetre.

2 Write the length indicated by each arrow to the nearest centimetre.

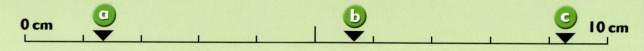

3 Work out, in metres, the distance between these arrows.

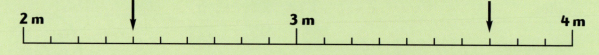

4 Add these lengths of cable.
Estimate the answers first,
by rounding to the nearest 10 cm.

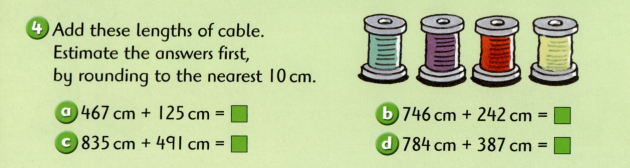

a 467 cm + 125 cm = ■
b 746 cm + 242 cm = ■
c 835 cm + 491 cm = ■
d 784 cm + 387 cm = ■

Let's investigate

5 Exact lengths of cable have been cut from the coil.
Investigate what the exact lengths could be if:

a Length A, rounded to the nearest 10 mm, is 5000 mm

b Length B, rounded to the nearest 10 cm, is 510 cm

c Length C, rounded to the nearest metre, is 6 m.

Let's solve problems

- The spacecraft is 500 m above the surface of the moon.
- The spaceman jumps from his craft to the moon.
- Each time he bounces back to 40% of his previous height.

For the first bounce, press these keys:

1 Copy and complete the table for 8 bounces.

Bounce	Calculation	Height
1	500 × 40%	200 m
2	200 × 40%	
3		
4		

2 After which bounce will he rise less than 1 m?

? What if the spacecraft was 300 m above the surface of the moon?

Let's solve problems

1 Copy and complete the table.
Write the mass of fruit in grams,
then balance each bag.
Use the fewest standard
masses possible.

Bag of apples 2 kg 650 g	Bag of peaches 3¼ kg

Bag of bananas 4·7 kg	Bag of oranges 5³⁄₁₀ kg	Bag of pears 6 kg 450 g

Bag	Mass in g	Standard masses used				
		1000 g	500 g	200 g	100 g	50 g
apples	2650 g	2	1	–	1	1
peaches						
bananas						
oranges						
pears						

2

Brie   Edam   Cheddar   Parmesan   Stilton

Use the table to find the mass of each piece of cheese.

Cheese	Standard masses used					
	500 g	200 g	100 g	50 g	20 g	10 g
Brie	1	–	1	–	1	1
Edam	1	2	–	1	–	2
Cheddar	–	3	1	–	3	1
Parmesan	4	–	1	1	–	4
Stilton	2	3	–	–	4	–

3 Work out the approximate mass of:

a 1 doughnut

b 1 Danish pastry

Let's practise

1 Write these capacities in millilitres.

> $3\frac{1}{4}$ l = 3000 ml + 250 ml = 3250 ml
>
> 3·25 l = 3000 ml + 250 ml = 3250 ml

a $3\frac{1}{2}$ l   **b** $5\frac{1}{4}$ l   **c** $2\frac{1}{10}$ l   **d** $4\frac{3}{4}$ l   **e** 6·5 l   **f** 8·7 l

g 2·01 l   **h** 4·06 l   **i** 0·75 l   **j** $7\frac{1}{5}$ l   **k** 9·33 l   **l** $9\frac{3}{5}$ l

Let's solve problems

2 **a** Copy and complete the table.
Use the recipe to find the missing quantities of lime juice or water.

Lime juice	Water
100 ml	400 ml
150 ml	
	1000 ml
330 ml	
	2 l
750 ml	
1·5 l	

Lime juice recipe

Measure 1 litre lime juice
and 4 litres water.
Mix well and serve chilled.

b How many litres of lime juice will you use with:
- 10 l of water
- 100 l of water?

c How many litres of water will you use with:
- 12 l of lime juice
- 120 l of lime juice?

3 You have 3 jugs.
You know the first holds 4 litres and the second holds 7 litres.
The third jug has a large capacity.
Explain how you will measure:

a 1 litre into the large jug

b 2 litres into the large jug.

Let's practise

1 Each water bottle holds 500 ml when full.
How many millilitres of water has each astronaut drunk?

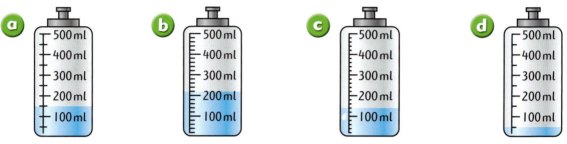

2 A shuttle craft starts with a full tank of fuel.
It makes 3 separate trips.
How much fuel is used on eah trip?

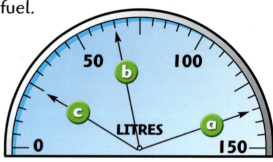

Let's solve problems

3 Jat has space sickness. He has to drink 350 ml of water 5 times a day.
The journey to planet Heras takes 3 days.
How many litres of water does he drink during the journey?

4 A space station has 1 million litres of fuel for its 250 space buggies.
Each buggy can only use its equal share of fuel.
How many litres is this?

Let's investigate

5 An alien makes drinks, but he only has 3 containers.
He draws a table to help him work out how to make different amounts.
Copy and complete the table up to 10 litres.

Amount	How the containers are used
1 litre	7 – 3 – 3
2 litres	12 – 7 – 3
3 litres	
4 litres	

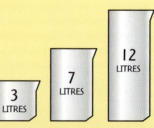

Let's practise

1 Copy and complete the table.

Pints	Millilitres	Litres
1	570 ml	0·57 l
2		
4		
8		
10		

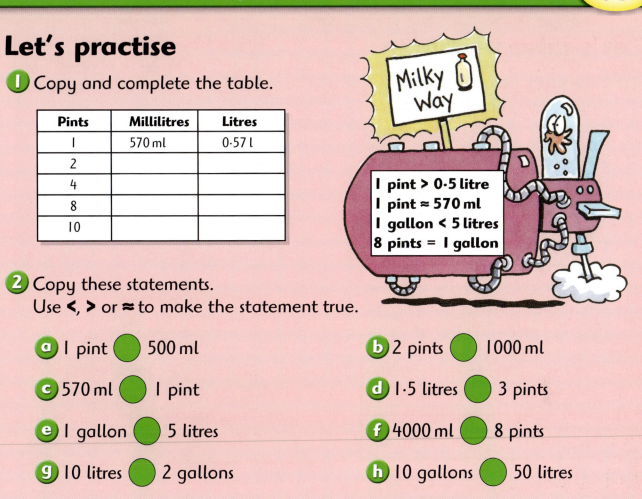

Milky Way

1 pint > 0·5 litre
1 pint ≈ 570 ml
1 gallon < 5 litres
8 pints = 1 gallon

2 Copy these statements.
Use **<**, **>** or **≈** to make the statement true.

a 1 pint ◯ 500 ml

b 2 pints ◯ 1000 ml

c 570 ml ◯ 1 pint

d 1·5 litres ◯ 3 pints

e 1 gallon ◯ 5 litres

f 4000 ml ◯ 8 pints

g 10 litres ◯ 2 gallons

h 10 gallons ◯ 50 litres

Let's solve problems

3 This is the weekly milk order for 2 families.

McDonalds

McKenzies

a Which family uses more milk in 1 week?
Find the approximate difference in millilitres.

b How long will it take the McDonalds to use 30 litres of milk?

c How long will it take the McKenzies to use 5 gallons of milk?

Let's solve problems

1 These black holes grow from the centre outwards.

a Copy and complete the table.

Square	Length of a side in cm	Perimeter in cm
black		
purple		
blue		
grey		

b Copy and complete the table.

Hexagon	Length of a side in cm	Perimeter in cm
black		
purple		
blue		
grey		

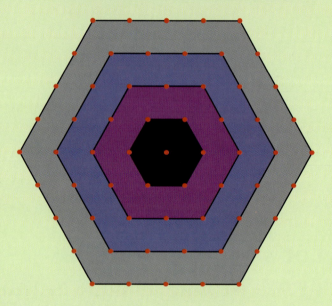

2 These black holes also grow in a pattern.

a Copy the table.

Square	1	2	3	4	5	6
Length of a side in cm	1·1					
Perimeter in cm						

Measure the sides of each square to the nearest millimetre.
Complete the table.

b Write about any patterns you notice in the table.

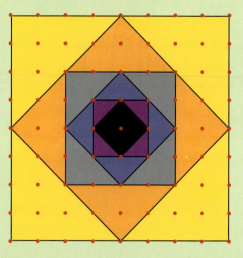

Let's practise

1 Find the areas of these rectangles in square centimetres.

a

b

c

2 **a** Draw a rectangle with an area of 24 cm^2.
What is the perimeter of your rectangle?

b Draw a rectangle with a perimeter of 24 cm.
What is the area of your rectangle?

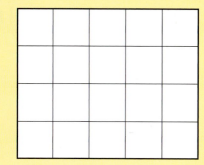

You need

I cm squared paper,
a ruler

Let's solve problems

3 Marco visited the NASA Space Center in Houston, Texas.
He made a display of the posters below on his bedroom wall.

- Find the area of each poster in cm^2.

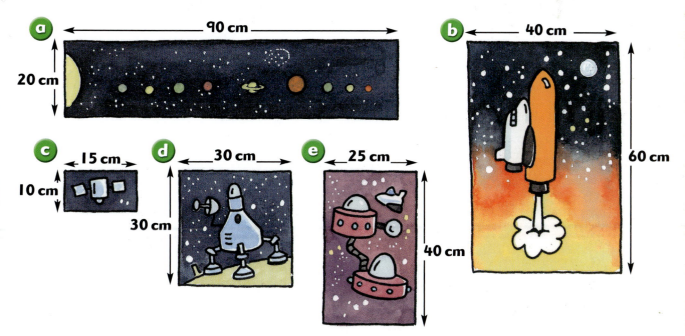

a 90 cm, 20 cm

b 40 cm, 60 cm

c 15 cm, 10 cm

d 30 cm, 30 cm

e 25 cm, 40 cm

- List the posters in order of area, starting with the smallest.

Let's practise

1. **a** Write the 12-hour and 24-hour times for each analogue clock.

To find 24-hour times, add 12 to pm times.

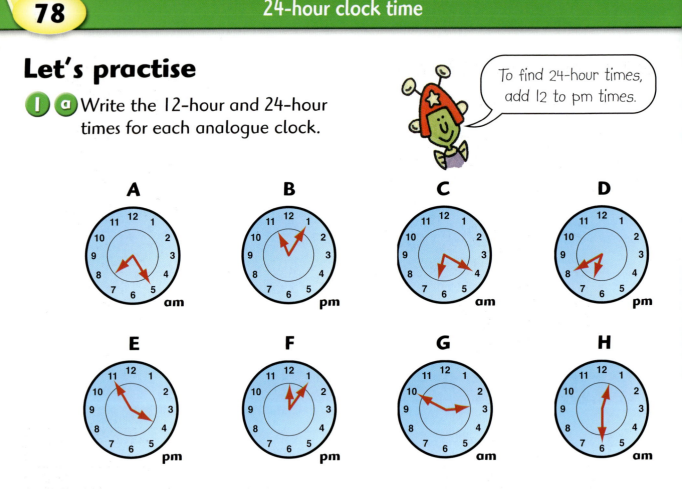

A am B pm C am D pm

E pm F pm G am H am

b Write the times above in order, starting with the earliest.

Let's solve problems

2. Vijay made this time line for his holiday flight to Orlando.

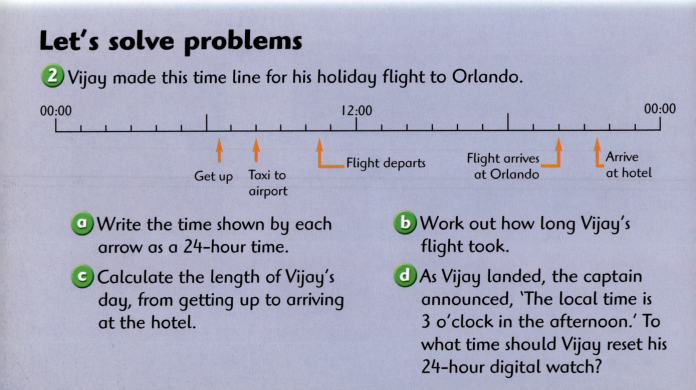

a Write the time shown by each arrow as a 24-hour time.

b Work out how long Vijay's flight took.

c Calculate the length of Vijay's day, from getting up to arriving at the hotel.

d As Vijay landed, the captain announced, 'The local time is 3 o'clock in the afternoon.' To what time should Vijay reset his 24-hour digital watch?

Let's solve problems

Departure times from moon base	
Moon buggy	leaves every 10 minutes
Space hopper	takes off every 12 minutes
Solar explorer	lifts off every 20 minutes

1 Copy and complete these timetables, using the table above.

a

Moon buggy	Time
1	08:00
2	08:10
3	
4	
5	
6	
7	
8	

b

Space hopper	Time
1	08:00
2	08:12
3	
4	
5	
6	
7	
8	

c

Space explorer	Time
1	08:00
2	08:20
3	
4	
5	
6	
7	
8	

2 The moon buggy, space hopper and space explorer all leave their launch pads together at 08:00.

What is the next time that they will all leave together?

Use the timetables to help you.

3 An interstellar rocket lifts off every 16 minutes.

The first flight each day is at 10:00 hours.

All 4 space vehicles leave together at 10:00.

What is the next time that they all leave their launch pads together?

Let's solve problems

Work with a partner.
On board the space shuttle, the pilot (P), the flight engineer (F) and the communications officer (C) had a discussion over who should go for meal breaks first.

You need

counters (in 4 different colours)

1 Copy and complete the rota so the astronauts take their meal breaks in a different order each day.

Check that your rota is fair and everyone has an equal chance of being first and last.

Day	Rota for meal breaks		
	1st	2nd	3rd
Monday	P	F	C
Tuesday			
Wednesday			

2 The space navigator (N) joined in the discussion.

a Copy and complete the rota for all 4 astronauts.

b Continue until your rota repeats itself.

Day	Rota for meal breaks			
	1st	2nd	3rd	4th
Monday	P	F	C	N
Tuesday				
Wednesday				

? What if there were 3 meal breaks a day and each lasted 45 minutes? Write a timetable to show when each astronaut could go for their meals on Monday.

Let's investigate

1 Pentominoes are made by joining 5 squares edge to edge. Some pentominoes will fold up to make an open cube.

You need

5 interlocking square tiles or squared paper

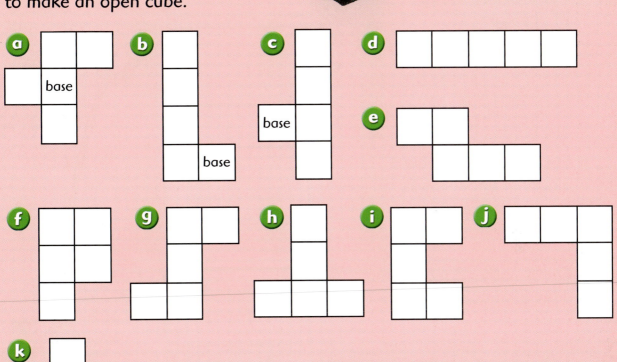

- Draw a table to record your results.
- Predict whether each pentomino is a net of an open cube or not.
- Make each pentomino.
- Check to test your prediction.

Pentomino	Prediction		Check	
	is a net	is not a net	is a net	is not a net
a	✓		✓	
b				
c				
d				
e				

? What if you used 6 squares to make hexominoes?

Let's solve problems

You need

2 sheets of A4 blank paper, ruler, sharp pencil, scissors, glue

1 ● Draw 4 rectangles
14 cm by 8 cm.
Put a tab on 1 edge
of each one.
Cut them out.

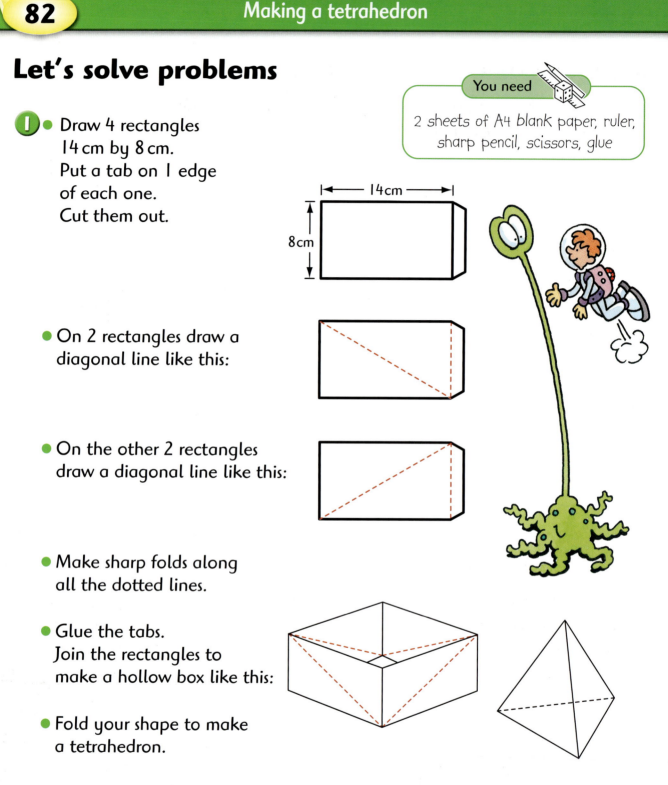

● On 2 rectangles draw a
diagonal line like this:

● On the other 2 rectangles
draw a diagonal line like this:

● Make sharp folds along
all the dotted lines.

● Glue the tabs.
Join the rectangles to
make a hollow box like this:

● Fold your shape to make
a tetrahedron.

? **a** What if you cut out and joined 4 rectangles 15 cm by 26 cm?
Will they fold to make a tetrahedron?

b Compare the width of the rectangle with the length of its diagonal.
Write about what you notice.

Let's practise

1 Write whether the purple lines are perpendicular or parallel.

perpendicular

a

b

c

d

e

f

g

h

2 Write whether the pairs of sides of the book are parallel or perpendicular to each other.

a AB and CD   b AC and BD

c AB and BD   d AC and AB

A   B

C   D

Let's play   A game for 2

● Player 1 chooses a polygon from the grid below.

● Player 2 guesses the name of the shape after asking questions to which the answer is 'Yes' or 'No'.

● If correct after 2 questions, score 3 points
       after 3 questions, score 2 points
       after 4 questions, score 1 point.

● The winner is the first player to score 10 or more points.

Is it a quadrilateral?
Does it contain one pair of parallel sides?
Does it have two pairs of perpendicular sides?

1   2   3   4   5

6   7   8   9   10

Let's solve problems

This is the space controller's screen monitor.
The dots show the distances of flying saucers
from Home Base and their flight paths.

Saucer Alpha calling Home Base.
My position is 3000 solar miles from
base. My flight path is 10°. Over.

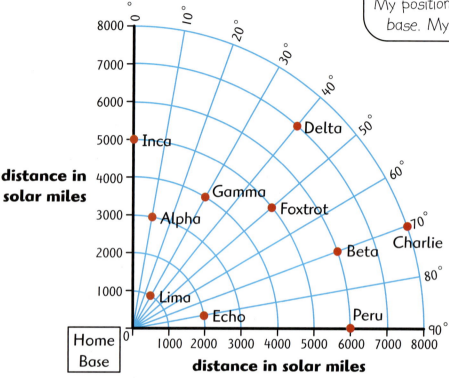

distance in solar miles

distance in solar miles

 Copy and complete the table for all the flying saucers.

Saucer	Distance in solar miles	Flight path
Alpha	3000	10°
Beta		
Charlie		
Delta		
Echo		

2 List the flying saucers in order, the one nearest to Home Base first.

3 Saucer Quito is on flight path 70°. It is closer to Home Base than
Saucer Charlie but further out than Saucer Gamma.
What might its position be?

Let's practise

1 Measure each angle to the nearest 5°.

You need

a protractor

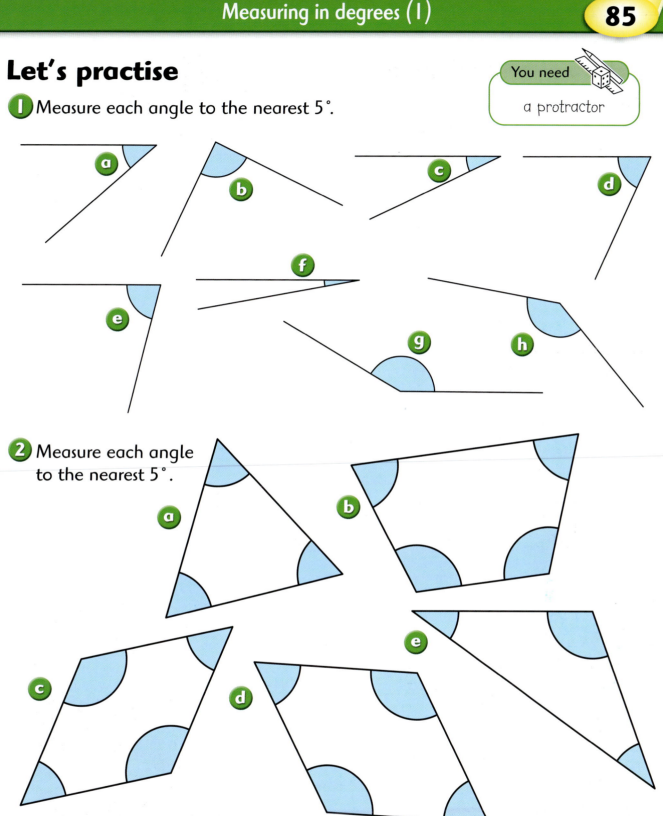

2 Measure each angle to the nearest 5°.

Let's investigate

3 Find the total of the angles in each triangle and quadrilateral in question 2. Write about what you notice.

Let's practise

1 Draw and label these angles:

a 40°   **b** 60°   **c** 75°   **d** 150°   **e** 125°   **f** 95°

> **You need**
> a protractor,
> a ruler

Let's solve problems

2 Calculate the size of the missing angle.

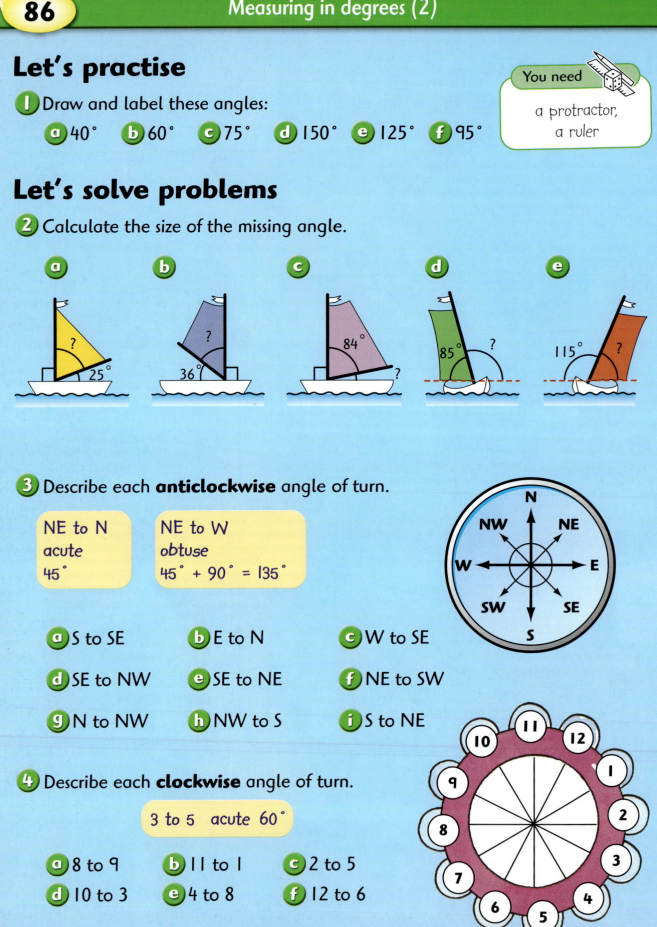

a   **b**   **c**   **d**   **e**

? 25°   ? 36°   84° ?   85° ?   115° ?

3 Describe each **anticlockwise** angle of turn.

> NE to N
> acute
> 45°

> NE to W
> obtuse
> 45° + 90° = 135°

a S to SE   **b** E to N   **c** W to SE

d SE to NW   **e** SE to NE   **f** NE to SW

g N to NW   **h** NW to S   **i** S to NE

4 Describe each **clockwise** angle of turn.

> 3 to 5   acute 60°

a 8 to 9   **b** 11 to 1   **c** 2 to 5

d 10 to 3   **e** 4 to 8   **f** 12 to 6

Let's practise

1 Copy and complete the table about numbers on the 100 square.

How many?	
Whole numbers	
Odd numbers	
Even numbers	
Numbers which end in 3	
Numbers which begin with 3	
Numbers where both digits are the same	
Numbers whose digits add up to 7	

1	2	3	4	5	6	7	8	9	10
11	12	13	14	15	16	17	18	19	20
21	22	23	24	25	26	27	28	29	30
31	32	33	34	35	36	37	38	39	40
41	42	43	44	45	46	47	48	49	50
51	52	53	54	55	56	57	58	59	60
61	62	63	64	61	66	67	68	69	70
71	72	73	74	75	76	77	78	79	80
81	82	83	84	85	86	87	88	89	90
91	92	93	94	95	96	97	98	99	100

Let's play   A game for 2

- Player 1 places 4 red and 3 blue cubes in the bag.
- Player 2 predicts which colour cube will be removed first.
- Player 1 removes a cube without looking in the bag, and shows it to player 2.
- If correct, player 2 keeps the cube. If incorrect, player 1 keeps the cube.
- Swap roles.

The winner is the player with more cubes after 3 rounds.

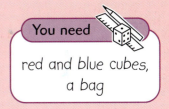

You need

red and blue cubes, a bag

? What if there were red, blue and green cubes?

Let's practise

1 Work out the total amounts for:

a 10  coins **b** 11 coins **c** 3 coins **d** 6 coins

e 9 coins **f** 18 coins **g** 15 coins **h** 23 coins

i 50 coins **j** 12 coins **k** 17 coins **l** 39 coins

Let's solve problems

	£2	£1	50p	20p	10p	5p	2p	1p
Sam	8	6	1	1	0	1	0	3
Jan	9	3	0	0	6	2	2	1
Tom	6	5	3	1	0	2	2	1
Sunil	5	8	2	1	3	1	1	3

2 The table shows the coins 4 children have saved.
Use the table to decide which of the following sentences are false.

a Sam has the most coins.

b Sam has the most money.

c Sunil has £19·60.

d Tom and Sunil have the same amount of money.

Let's investigate

3 Investigate different ways of making £2·50 using no more than 6 coins.
Use £2, £1, 50p, 20p and 10p coins only. Record your findings.

A table may help.

? What if you used the same coins to make £3?
Would there be more or fewer ways?

Let's solve problems

1 Some children did a test.
There were 20 questions.
Here are their marks.

16	20	11	15	18	17	17	18
19	17	16	18	17	17	19	18
16	15	19	20	17	17	16	16
18	17	19	17	18	17	19	15

Copy and complete the frequency table to record the marks.

Score	Tally	Frequency
11	I	
12		

2 Use your table to answer these questions.

a How many children scored less than 16?

b How many scored 17 or over?

c Do you think that the children found the test
easy or difficult? Explain your answer.

d What was the most common score?

This is called the mode

? What if these were the answers to some
questions about the frequency table?

• 5

• none

• 1

What could the questions have been?

Let's practise

1 Pete asked children at his school which fruit they liked best. Here is a bar line chart of the results.

Write True or False for each of these statements:

a Pete asked 40 children.

b Two more children voted for strawberries than voted for apples.

c A vote for kiwi fruit may have been included on the chart.

d You can tell from this chart that these children eat more strawberries than apples.

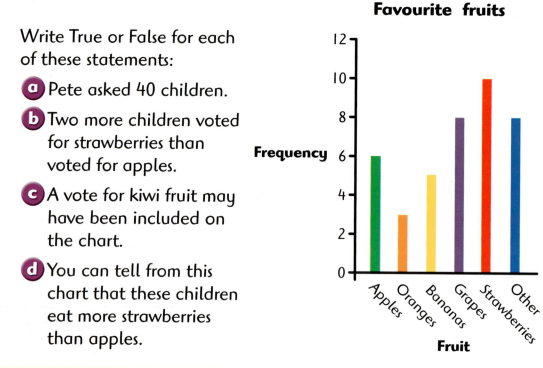

Favourite fruits

Let's investigate

Work with a partner.
Toni and Kai play a game of Space hoppers.
They use an ordinary dice. They must roll a 6 to start.

Kai says: I am less likely to roll a 6 than any other number.

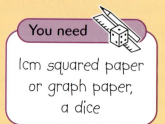

You need

1cm squared paper or graph paper, a dice

2 a Do you think this statement is true?

b Roll a dice 50 times and record the results in a frequency table.

3 a Draw a bar line chart of your results.

b Was 6 the number that was rolled least often?

c Were your results what you expected? Explain.

? What if you rolled the dice another 50 times?

Let's solve problems

1 Rob and Amy get the same amount of pocket money each week.
Once a month Rob checks how much money he has and records
the amount in a graph. Amy does the same.

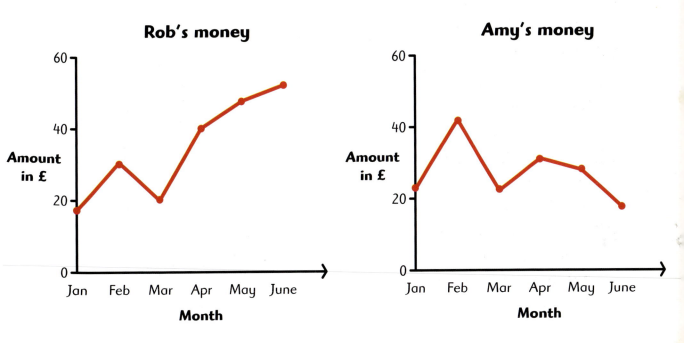

a Who started the year with more money?

b Who managed to save more?

c In which months did they both record about the same amount?

d Between which 2 months did the amount Rob have decrease?

e About how much more money did Amy record in February than in March?

f In June, about how much more did Rob have than Amy?

? What if Rob earns some extra money by starting a paper round in July?
Draw a graph to show that by Christmas he has earned enough to buy
a new bike costing £245.

Let's investigate

Use tally marks to record.

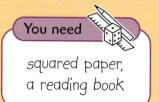

You need

squared paper, a reading book

1 **a** Look at the first 5 lines in a reading book. Predict which letter will appear most often. Do not count them.

b Look at the lines again, this time recording the total number of times each letter appears in a tally chart.

c Use the information to make a graph or chart on squared paper.

d Which letter is the mode?

e Write down the 5 most common letters in order.

f Are there any letters that do not occur? What are they?

g Compare your graph or chart with someone else's.

Mode means the most common.

2 Look at the next 5 lines in the book and compile a graph or chart. Compare your results with the first 5 lines.

? What if you used your results to predict how many of each letter there might be on 1 whole page of your book? Check your prediction.